PRAISE FOR
STAND IN YOUR SPOTLIGHT

"Jenni's story is a rollicking life journey of courage, determination, and adaptability. A brilliant collection of experiences lived and shared, reinventions foreseen and executed, and challenges faced and conquered. We can all see glimpses of ourselves within it and take inspiration from it as we shape our own futures."
—Rt. Hon. Dame Jenny Shipley, DNZM,
Former Prime Minister of New Zealand

"Jenni's journey of resilience is woven through the fabric of this uplifting story, which chronicles the challenges women face and the strength they find in overcoming them. I first met Jenni when she served as chair of the San Diego County Commission on the Status of Women and Girls, and even then, I knew her wisdom and caring spirit would take her far and inspire others along the way. This book does exactly that."
—California Senate President Pro Tempore Toni G. Atkins

"Jenni Prisk's book *Stand in Your Spotlight* should be read by every man who wants to have a meaningful relationship with a woman. She opens her heart and soul to her readers. We need to understand the importance of equality."
—Phil Blair, Executive Officer, Manpower San Diego

"Beneath Jenni's gentle persuasion of all women to take advantage of every opportunity, she emphatically urges us to keep talking and seize the spotlight by using our collective voices to shout out for equality, justice, and peace. Her message is powerful: seize the spotlight, create the change."

—Anne Hoiberg, Past President, Women's Museum of California, League of Women Voters, and United Nations Association-USA, San Diego

"You've heard of coming-of-age stories. Well, *Stand in Your Spotlight* is a coming-of-voice story. Jenni Prisk shares her own remarkable journey in finding power and passion through her voice. She reminds us all how important it is to stand in our own power and live to our fullest potential. Inspiring, touching, and motivating, this book will help us all access our inner strength and resilience. Jenni reminds us that life is not what happens to us, but how we choose to react to it. *Stand in Your Spotlight* is exactly the book we need right now to remember that we can be powerful and we can make a difference, even in our toughest times."

—Lorri Sulpizio, PhD, Director, Conscious Leadership Academy, School of Leadership and Education Sciences, University of San Diego

"Jenni Prisk is an amazing woman whose story of passion, resilience, and resourcefulness makes one admire her even more. Despite a tormented childhood—which led to self-doubt and excruciating despair—she turned her demons into positive life lessons and took center stage. The intimacy of Jenni's candor and the wisdom she imparts are at the heart of this compelling read."

—Karin Winner, former Editor, San Diego *Union-Tribune*, Philanthropist

"From the preface to the epilogue, Jenni's book sings. Her prose is at once intimate and effusive. She speaks directly from her heart to the reader, confronting taboo subjects fearlessly and honestly, eliciting a deeply emotional response. Jenni has crafted a very wise book on the many joys and pains on the journey of life."

—Dr. Emily Murase, award-winning champion of women's empowerment as Former Director of the San Francisco Department on the Status of Women

AN ODE TO LIVING FULLY

STAND
IN YOUR
SPOTLIGHT

JENNI PRISK

Printed and bound in the United States of America
ISBN: 978-0-578-31521-8
Library of Congress Control Number: 2021923013

DEDICATION

To all the women in the world; keep fighting the good fight.
To Kim, my strength and stay.

All the world's a stage,
And all the men and women merely players;
They have their exits and their entrances;
And one man in his time plays many parts,
His acts being seven ages.

—*As You Like It*,
William Shakespeare

CONTENTS

Seventh Decade: Becoming

PREFACE

Why have I written a book about my life? I'm a regular person, living a regular life. I'm not a celebrity or a star or an intellectual maven that the world knows. I have three reasons for the book: to share lessons learned and blunders to avoid, to embolden your self-esteem, and to inspire you to be your best self.

A friend heard me deliver a speech about my life and urged me to write this book. "You have inspirational lessons for women, especially those who doubt their abilities, or who are being held back by the past and can't move into the present." That was enough for me, and so the process began. During COVID. In New Zealand. In 2020.

As you turn the pages, I hope you'll see yourself on some of them; that you'll be reminded of the accomplishments and setbacks that shaped the person you are today. Perhaps you'll read a line that resonates with something you've done today, or yesterday, that will help you tomorrow. I also hope you'll smile when you recognize similar struggles that we've both overcome.

I encourage you to reflect on your courage, resilience, and achievements; that you'll seize every positive opportunity in your own life. Discard the negatives that hold you back. Focus on the benefits that will move you forward on your journey.

Confidence is paramount to your success. According to the 2021 Women's Confidence Index, developed after researching 11,176 women in 11 countries, confidence serves the same purpose for all of us: to facilitate social-assimilation. And that means being accepted for who we are.

My book is written with love and caring for the human psyche. We are fragile beings, as we have seen when Olympic or sports heroes plummet to the depths. We don't really know why some succeed and others don't. All we know is that every one of them has given their utmost. As do we in our daily lives.

In my early decades, I never dreamed that I would create a business, develop a nonprofit organization, live in America, or travel the world. But I took advantage of every opportunity, and I continue to do so. Our state of life is determined by our state of mind.

Women are a powerful, empowering sex, yet can be sabotaged through self-doubt. We must think up, and out, to the edges of our strengths and abilities. We must recognize our fortitude and passion as tools for sustainability. And growth. And not bypass the possibilities that are afforded us because we lack self-esteem or belief in ourselves.

As Nicholas Kristof of the *New York Times* said: "Women hold up half the sky." We must take our equal leadership on the global stage and make our presence felt. Use. Our. Voices. For the betterment of the planet. For the betterment of ourselves. This poem I wrote expresses my sentiments:

It's not about the shape of our parts,
It's about the size of our hearts.
Its not about the swing in our hips,
It's what we utter with our lips.

It's not about the color of our eyes,
It's what we see when we rise,
It's not about the color of our skin,
It's what we do with what's within.

Activating Woman, your time has come!
To uplift and inspire this great nation!
Put aside all doubts and fears,
Dry your eyes, and no more tears!

There's work to do, and it's women's work,
Activate! And never shirk!
We must speak out and use our voices
Otherwise, we'll lose our choices
    to be free, strong, and motivated.
Rise up! Let's get activated!

We may never meet, yet my hope for you is that something in my book inspires you to be the very best you can be, no matter where you live, how you live, or what you dream. Life isn't a dress rehearsal. It's "curtain up" every day as we are invited to give the performance of our lives. Stand in your spotlight, listen for the applause, and acknowledge the accolades. They are for you.

Acknowledgments

A book cannot be written without the support and commitment of many.

To Bethany Kelly of *Publishing Partner* who suggested I write down my experiences. She has been with me every step of the way to shape, design, and coax this book out of me. I am deeply grateful.

To my business colleagues and clients in San Diego and the United States, who, over the years, have insisted that I write a book—well, here it is! I've finally written it. Thank you all for your encouragement. Special thanks to Karin Winner, former editor of the San Diego *Union-Tribune,* who nurtured my writing. And to Phil Blair of Manpower who continues to advise me.

To the special friends mentioned in the book. Your love and our memories always inspire me.

To the friends not named, in San Diego, New Zealand, and around the globe, thank you for your constancy.

To my maternal grandmother, who was a huge influence in my life. She emanated strength and fortitude, underlined by the importance of a positive attitude. I hope I'm like her.

To the teachers at junior and high school who imbued in me a love of words, theatre, and travel. I am grateful! And I listened to you more than you may have guessed!

To the board of Voices of Women, who for almost two decades believed in our mission to empower and support women globally.

To the women in business, in nonprofits, in NGOs, in leadership, and to those living in hardship who continually inspire me to be a better version of myself.

To all those who have overcome adversity, hatred, persecution, and loss, I acknowledge you.

To those who may not be mentioned here, yet who have been positive role models in my life, thank you. You live in towns and cities that span the globe. You know who you are.

To my family in New Zealand who I love beyond measure.

And to Kim, who has been there for me, believed in me, and loved me for forty-plus years.

First Decade

1949–1959

Arriving

REFLECTIONS

The curtain rises. There you are. Young, small, bewildered, yet safe in this new world. Billions came before you. Billions will follow. But none will ever be like you.

You've arrived with a blank canvas. The world will write on that canvas, but you will have the final word. The space is yours.

You've joined a family of three—another daughter. A sister for the one who is already nine years old. There would have been a son, but he died before he was born and is never mentioned.

Your role is to bring love and laughter to a sometimes-tense household. To become the focus of a loving mother and an enigmatic father who have stamped your DNA. Enjoy the love that is provided in your new home, but be wary. There are dangers ahead that will affect your mind and body. There will also be joy through activities, friendship, and family. In these early years you will simply be a little girl who wants to be loved and protected. And you will be, until the shadows fall and the stage that was set for you begins to crumble at the edges. And not all the characters on the stage have good intentions.

Learn to love yourself. Build your fortress. Step into the spotlight. Your life begins.

CHAPTER 1

'Tis the eye of childhood that fears a painted devil.
Macbeth

I t's one of those summer days that shimmers. Butterflies, bees, and birds are busy in the garden. The sun casts a warm glow. The intoxicating perfume from the flowering shrubs in our sprawling section fills the air. Our single-story home is simple and modest, on a quiet, tree-lined street in suburban Christchurch, New Zealand. It's 1951.

On this tranquil day, I'm wearing a white dress with blue smocking. I'm two years old. A photograph captures the moment I pick up a corner of the dress's hem and twirl on the rug that's been laid out for a picnic on the lawn. How I love to dance! And talk! I jabber constantly, commenting on everything. "Look at the butterfly," "smell the pretty flower," and "I'm hungry," a frequent lament!

My mother, father, and older sister are in the garden too. We don't have a lot of money; however, life is comfortable. We picnic on Sundays or visit my grandmother and other family members who live in Christchurch. The Korean War is in progress and the country is recovering from World War II and the ensuing depression. These experiences don't impact the life of a child, especially if the household is happy, which mine seems to be.

About this time in my life, Mum takes me to meet with a small group of doctors. They sit me on a table and surround me. I love an audience! I can count higher than ten and speak in full sentences. The local pharmacist had suggested to my mother that I be "checked out." For what, I'm not exactly sure!

The doctors ask me a series of questions. According to Mum, I answered them all clearly. At the end of the "interview," the doctors recommended: "Be sure to seek advanced learning for Jennifer when she starts school." "Read to her a lot, and make sure she reads aloud." "Encourage her to keep talking!" Holy cow, that final comment isn't necessary. My chatter's already incessant! Some days, Mum has to ask me to sit quietly and read a book so she can get some peace and quiet.

Years later, when Mum and I talked about the experience, she told me she wished she'd pursued the doctors' counsel to seek out augmented education. She didn't, and I frolicked my way through my school years, happy not to have to work too hard. There are times when I'm curious about who I might have become had she followed their advice. So often others perceive skills in us that we don't acknowledge or appreciate.

Language and languages fascinated me. I remember one occasion when I was about four, Mum and I took the bus to town to do some shopping, a very exciting treat. On this ride there were two passengers speaking in a foreign accent. I tugged at my mother's sleeve as we alighted from the bus.

"Can we please follow them?" I pleaded.

Mum looked uncertain, and somewhat cross. "We're not going their way."

"Pleeease!"

She relented, and for several blocks we walked behind the strangers. I concentrated on their voices. That evening, I practiced their accents.

That same year at Christmas, Mum and I went to town to visit the beautiful Gothic cathedral that graced the center of Christchurch. I clutched a favorite doll which I'd dressed in her best clothes. Her name was Merle. I wrote a note and pinned it inside the doll's jacket. As we walked up the cathedral aisle, my heart began to quake. Could I really part with my beloved friend? I gently placed Merle among the gifts under the Christmas tree. My gift to a child who had less than I did. I wept silent tears on the way home. Mum had offered to buy a toy so that I wouldn't have to give Merle away. But I was determined that another child would receive something I had loved. What was this early altruism about? Did I have a generous heart, or was I just being a martyr? What urged me to self-sacrifice? Was it the guilt that would plague me for most of my life?

It's interesting to reflect on my early propensities: a need to express myself, a love of foreign patois, and a burgeoning desire to help others. The building blocks of my identity were taking shape. But so was an underlying menace.

11

When I turned five, I was excited to start school. New friends, new discoveries, and a permanent audience! On the first day, I was apprehensive and teary at leaving Mum, but as soon as I met up with the other kids in my classroom, my fears were dispelled. Some of them were struggling more than I was, so I comforted and took care of them. The teachers thought it was very kind; I think I was just a bossy kid!

Eventually, I was allowed to walk to school with the lovely boy who lived next door. James was seven years old, very serious and responsible, and Mum knew I'd be safe with him. She and his mother were close friends. I well remember them drinking copious cups of tea, smoking their heads off, and exchanging gossip.

"I'll come and sit with you at lunchtime," James said as he delivered me to my classroom door. And he did religiously for the first week. His attentions stopped when he saw that I was having fun cavorting in the playground with new friends.

I giggled and fooled my way through the early years at school. Learning came easily, so I guess I thought that gave me license to act up, mimic the teachers, and be the loudest voice in the class. My favorite time of the school day was reading. I especially loved being asked to read passages aloud to the whole class. Expression, theatrics, and words were my best friends. Little did I know that those friends would follow me all the days of my life!

So, where's my father in all this? I haven't mentioned him till now. Like most fathers of the era, he was hands-off in raising me. He just loved cuddling me, touching my hair, and telling me what a beautiful little girl I was. "I'll never forget how you looked when you were born. I could have eaten you up, you were so gorgeous," was one of his favorite statements. Why did this always make me feel uncomfortable? He didn't say these things to my sister. Why me? Over the next several years I would find out.

CHAPTER 2

Of all base passions, fear is most accursed.
Henry VI, Part I

Mum suffered from severe migraines. When they struck, she took to her bed for a few days in a darkened room, barely able to move. I hated seeing her in pain and felt it was my job to take care of her. While I sat in the dark holding her hand, she would whisper, "Go outside and play," but I wouldn't.

For reasons then unknown to me, I had to be her protector. Dad would come home from work and not go near her. That seemed very strange to me. My sister and I would cook dinner and eat it with Dad, without much conversation. There was uneasiness at that table that made my stomach turn.

I'd become obsessed with ballet and used to devour every book about the art that I could find. For hours I'd pirouette around our lounge, watching myself in a big mirror while I dreamed of my future as a prima ballerina. When I turned

14

seven, my mother enrolled me in ballet classes at the local YWCA. I thought I'd died and was on my way to heaven! The magical world of dance swept me away as I imagined a future filled with tutus and toe shoes.

When I danced, the demons disappeared. What demons? I was never entirely sure. I just knew I felt safe and free while moving, not having to face the uncomfortable quiet that frequently pervaded our house.

One of my friends in the neighborhood, Adele, started ballet classes with me. She was blonde and petite. I was tall and solidly built. One look at the two of us and you could guess who wouldn't make it into the corps de ballet! Yet my passion for dance was steadfast. I practiced every plié and jeté with fervor. And when I graduated to toe shoes, at age eleven, my cup runneth over. (Looking back, the number of hours I spent "en pointe" probably caused the broken toes I have today!)

I slept, dreamt, ate, talked, and breathed ballet. When Margot Fonteyn and Michael Somes came to dance in Christchurch in 1959 (I was ten), I saved so hard for my ticket that I was able to pay for Mum's too. I can still vividly remember the lights going down in the Christchurch Theatre Royal and two ethereal images floating onto the stage. I joined the Fonteyn fan club and wrote to her, receiving a signed, autographed photo which lived under my pillow until it was in tatters.

My ballet class put on a performance to which our parents were invited. Only my mother came, as she always did. My father, never. I would plead, but he was always "otherwise engaged."

"I have to have a 'tutu' for the show," I told Mum. Money was tight, so my mother (who wasn't a seamstress) decided to make one for me. It was pink, with a satin bodice and some pearls. I thought it was heavenly until I saw the others at rehearsal. A tutu is made of short stiff layers of nylon netting, attached to frilly knickers. The netting is supposed to sit up and out from the waist. Mine hung down nearly to my knees. It looked droopy, and so did I. My spirits were lifted when the lovely dance teacher explained, "Jennifer, yours is a 'romantic' tutu." Her kind remark worked wonders.

The older I grew, the more I realized that money was a *big* issue in our household. There was even less of it than I thought. My father was a frivolous spender, and even though my sister and I weren't deprived of anything necessary, we sensed the shortage when our parents had heated discussions about their finances. They had separate checking accounts and would barter down to the last penny who was paying which bill. Those darned money issues plagued me for most of my life. And on many occasions, they limited my thinking and development.

There was a great deal of unease in our home. Dad would sometimes go for two or three days without speaking, isolating himself in his shed, eating his meals alone, going for long drives alone in the family car. It was creepy! I think this was the reason I liked to play at other kids' houses. Their families seemed different. I knew something was wrong at home. And there were things wrong with me too. My stomach was in constant turmoil. I had vivid, frightening nightmares of large, upright dragons with fiery mouths that lived in my closet. I developed whooping cough and wheezed my way through many sleepless nights. Mum was a gentle nurse; My sister would sit on my bed and tell me about her day, which I loved. Dad only stopped by my room to stroke my head or touch me in ways that were subversive and unhealthy.

My sister, who is nine years older than me, was a very attractive young woman. She was pursued by an assorted variety of young men who made a fuss over me when they called, much to her annoyance! She went on skating and skiing and boating trips with them, which left me at home alone with my parents. I began to realize what a safety buffer she was for me.

To help pass the time in her absence, I wrote short plays and performed them for Mum and Dad. I placed two chairs side by side to try to get my parents to sit closely together, but try as I might, it didn't work, and they drew increasingly apart.

When the strain at home got tough, Mum would tell me, "You and I are going to Wellington to stay with your aunt. You'll be going to school with your cousin while we're there. Won't that be exciting?!"

It was all a big adventure for me, but I could feel the underlying worry and sadness. We were escaping the situation at home in Christchurch, while my sister, who was working by now, was left to tough it out with Dad.

By this time, Mum and Dad were sleeping in separate rooms, something I hated. I wanted my family to be "normal." A creeping sense of fear had begun to invade my body. The stomach complaints frequently sent me to the bathroom.

One evening, a very special young man arrived for dinner. He and my sister dated and married and had four children. He was my brother-in-law for 58 years, until his death in 2020. Just before the wedding, Mum found a note from my father on the dining room table that told of an affair he'd been having. It wasn't the first. My father was a philanderer and a charmer.

Mum and I went to stay with an uncle and aunt in Christchurch, to get away from the turmoil. I'll never forget

Mum's question in the taxi on the way home, "What do you want me to do about your father?"

"I want him to come home," I said, tearfully.

So, he did. And that was the start of a near lifetime of guilt for me about Mum, her health, and her happiness.

Life, when Dad returned, was more strained than ever. My stomach was in knots all the time. Another friend in our street went to a Catholic school in the area. One day she took me to her chapel. Upon entering, I saw the most exquisite statue of the Virgin Mary.

I got down on my knees and started praying to her to "save me." And then another phrase forced its way into my head. "Don't let me kill her." Where had that phrase come from? My father? And who was the "her?" In horror, I realized it was Mum! I wasn't a killer, was I? Why would I keep repeating those appalling words?

CHAPTER 3

Every one can master a grief but he that has it.
Much Ado About Nothing

My sister's wedding was fabulous. I wore a long blue satin gown, long white gloves (that didn't really fit my pudgy arms), and my hair was primped into its best curls. The party at home afterwards went on till the wee small hours, and I couldn't have been happier to have so many friends and relatives in the house. But the happiness was short-lived.

The happy couple were away on their honeymoon when one evening I began weeping bitterly in my bedroom. My sister was gone. Her presence in the house was a calming influence when the atmosphere was tense. She was the family member I could turn to in times of turmoil.

"What's the matter, why are you crying?" Mum asked.

When I told her, she reprimanded me. "Well, I'm missing her terribly too."

And that was that. I had to mourn my sister's departure in silence and let all those emotions churn inside me.

My period started when I was eleven. Sadly, I didn't know what was going on, as the topic had never been raised at home. When it showed up in my knickers in the restroom of a large Christchurch department store, I thought I was dying. It took me two days to tell Mum, who told me that I was "growing up." To my embarrassment, she told Dad, which elicited from him, "You're a woman now." That should have been a compliment, but it scared me.

When my sister and her husband returned from their honeymoon, we made up a double bed for them in the spare room. I kept asking Mum, "Why are they allowed to sleep together?" I never got a straight answer. I hoped Mum would tell me about sex, but she replied, "You know those people in Africa who have a lot of babies? Well, it's what happens when a man and a woman get close." *That* was helpful! So, the rest of my sex education came from the kids at school, who told hair-raising stories about the act that put me off for years!

As I moved into the second decade of my life, exciting changes took place, but there were also shocks and surprises, some of which would shape my future for years. While I didn't understand what was going on in my head or happening to my body, I knew things weren't right. Sitting at the dining table with my parents, struggling to swallow, running to the bathroom during a meal, finding I couldn't breathe properly, and starting to sweat when I was in a room alone with Dad. Was this normal? Were other kids experiencing this too? I didn't know, because I never asked and certainly didn't tell.

SECOND DECADE

1959–1969

LEARNING

REFLECTIONS

So, now you're in your learning years, in this second decade of your life. Time to test those abilities and appetites. You'll try a lot of things, and not all of them will work. The discoveries and mistakes you make will shape you for your future. It'll be exciting and enticing, and scary too. Learning is a lifelong treat, but you don't know that yet. You're taking one step at a time. And fortunately, life isn't all exams!

Another great thing you'll learn about is friendship. How to make friends and how to keep them. Usually through shared values, but you don't fully understand how important they are yet. You just know when you feel secure being with someone, especially the laughing moments. And when you're part of a "gang" of friends, you can conquer the world.

You'll be discovering what your body parts are for. And kissing, and sex, and flirting, and all that other stuff that they write songs and make movies about.

You're also starting to see your parents as people. You begin to realize that they don't just put food on the table, sheets on your bed, or hustle you to study. They're people with foibles, and fears, and maybe some strange habits. And you might not like everything you see. Especially if they don't communicate with each other very well. Or don't get along the way you'd like them to. Please, please, don't get caught in the middle. Their battles aren't yours to fight. You'll have enough of your own. Keep a clear-eyed vision on the road ahead.

CHAPTER 4

The instruments of darkness tell us truths.
Macbeth

My sister had a family quickly and I was over the moon about these new young lives in our midst. I spent nearly every school holiday with them. As the children grew, my time was filled with tons of activities: taking the kids to school and back and often to the beach, doing laundry, cooking, gardening, planting vegetables, and crashing early into bed each night. My sister was amazing with all that she accomplished. I romped freely through those years, relishing every moment with her kids. They were like the younger siblings I'd always wanted.

My mother was resentful of the time I spent away, because it left her at home alone with Dad. They did visit and sometimes stayed over a weekend. One day when Mum and I returned to Christchurch from a weekend with my sister, as I was carrying her things into the house, two of the children who lived down the street from my parents burst in through the back door.

"Hello," one exclaimed. "We slept in your bed last night."

The blood froze in my veins. Mum and I went into shock. The sunny day turned gray. God in heaven, what had my father done?

He had offered to "babysit" the children, to give their parents a night off. "Why don't you let them sleep over," he had said with his usual charm. Never mentioning that my mother wasn't at home.

Why did this feel menacing? Couldn't this just be a kind gesture? Why was my stomach in turmoil? Was it because of all the inappropriate touching I had experienced from my father?

I was the one who spoke to the parents, imploring them to never allow the children to visit again. I rang the family doctor and lawyer to see if anything could be done about Dad's behavior. Both advised that the only way they could lay any penalty on my father would be if he was "caught in the act." In the act of what, exactly? I knew something was seriously wrong. My personal recollections and memories told me that something sinister was stirring.

When challenged about his behavior, he locked himself in his bedroom and wouldn't come out or speak to us. The atmosphere in the house was hideous. Mum and I crept around as though the fault was ours. The hours and days went by as we tried to keep a sense of calm and normality. I was so concerned about the children that I put my fears aside—they would catch up with me later!

Mum didn't want any of this mentioned outside our home. In the 1960s, sexual predation was not discussed publicly. It was shaming and shocking. And Mum had a reputation to uphold. She was very principled and determined that her circle wouldn't know about the circumstances behind our doors. The image she wanted others to see was that she'd married a man from a wealthy family and life was good! It was not! It was becoming very unhealthy.

In her marriage, Mum was more like a chattel than a wife. She was afraid of my father. He didn't physically abuse her; however, his physical strength alarmed her. She held a notion that if she died first, he would fill the house with women and they would laugh at her, over her casket! This made me determined that if I ever married, I'd want an equal partnership with a man who respected and honored me!

CHAPTER 5

To climb steep hills requires a slow pace at first.
Henry VIII

A whole new way of life entered mine ... high school! I desperately wanted to attend Avonside Girls' High because my sister went there. My primary (junior) schoolteachers had recommended that I take a professional course, which focused on language, so I was ecstatic. However, I had to take math too, which was a real bummer. I chose shorthand and typing as my elective topics so I could become a secretary, despite advice from people smarter than me who suggested I teach. The thought of teaching made me want to barf. Little did I know that in years to come, one of the greatest pleasures in my life would come from that profession!

The first day in the classroom was chaotic as we girls tried to work out where we would sit. I was a self-conscious teenager, overweight and insecure. No one, I thought, would want to sit with me. I was drawn to a petite, blond, blue-eyed girl who stood shyly off to the side.

"Could I sit with you?" I asked, tentatively.

"Yes, please," she eagerly replied.

"I'm Jennifer," I said.

"I'm Vy," she said, smiling.

And that was the start of a beautiful friendship that continues today.

Vy lived near my home, so we biked to school together, rain or shine. Both of us had older sisters and no brothers, so we loved to vary our route past the boys' high school to see who we could spot. Our favorite pastime was giggling, which got us into trouble in the classroom on many occasions. I was usually the punished protagonist as my voice was stronger and louder than Vy's. My clowning in class continued throughout my years in high school, but it soothed my soul when everyone (sometimes even the teachers) laughed at my mimicry or sense of humor. I was frequently sent to the principal's office, who I don't think ever thought I was bad. I remember her hiding a smile when I described some of the antics that led me to the seat on the other side of her desk.

Clowns can be the saddest creatures on the planet. Constant joking and craving the limelight sometimes has a flip side, especially if there's crying involved. My family, who were used to my "entertaining" nature, used to laugh when my tears followed. They made comments like "there she goes again" or "here comes the drama."

I wish they'd asked me some specific questions. Are you happy at school? Do you feel safe at home? Are your friends treating you well? Do you feel as though you belong? Is there anything we can do to help? I needed help but didn't know exactly what for. It had been made clear to me that my needs weren't the most important in our home. Also, being a clown means there's a reputation to uphold. I had to stay in charge of my game.

Through my years at high school I excelled at Latin, French, and English. Languages! I loved history too, primarily because our teacher had a yacht, and one afternoon each month he took our class out to the local estuary and taught us how to sail in his old tub of a boat. I don't know how he wrangled it. I think he must have told the principal that he would teach us about the high seas, or ancient boating, or something historical. The sailing was wonderful, except when we forgot to check on low tide and had to pull the boat back into the jetty, on foot, through the mud.

How I hated math! Fortunately, Vy did too, and we endured some of our classes by writing scathing notes and passing them back and forth to each other. When Mum saw my poor exam results, James, the boy next door, was invited to coach me. Poor guy, that was a mistake. He was in his final year at high school, heading to university to take an engineering degree, when he assumed the dreaded role. I can still see him banging his head against the wall of our sitting room when the square root of the hypotenuse wouldn't register in my unwilling brain!

When we sat our school certificate exams in our third year, Vy and I arrived at the math exam half an hour later than the required time. We had legitimately got it wrong. We sat across the room from each other but had practiced a coughing routine. One cough meant "I'm going to read the paper one more time to see if there's a question I can answer." Two coughs meant "I'm sick to death of this paper!" And three coughs meant "I'm done!" On a double set of three coughs, we handed in our papers and discreetly left the room. We leapt on our bikes and spent the rest of the afternoon splashing in the ocean. Our parents really should have blasted us for this behavior. Unfortunately, they didn't!

When the results came back, I had scored nine percent, and Vy got eleven (without a coach)! To this day, we can't work out how she got two more marks than me! However, we both got the certificate, so we were happy. And, a few years later, I arranged a blind date for her with James. They've been happily married for fifty years and counting.

My parents weren't academic. School was a place I had to attend, rather than an institution in which I could flourish. I wish they'd told me about their classes and studies. Instead, all I knew was that Mum had been a swimming champion and Dad had run away from boarding school.

I loved the sporting activities at school. The movement, physicality, and camaraderie were elements I pursued with vigor. My mother's swimming and Dad's early years of gym instruction infused the importance of physical activity in me. Not that I was outstanding at my favorite sports of netball, tennis, swimming, and "rounders" (a form of baseball), but I played with everything I had. Being busy and engaged kept me sane, and away from home in the evenings when I had practice. But there was another "sport" in the wings that would reveal itself soon.

CHAPTER 6

The play's the thing …
Hamlet

I n my fourth year at high school, an activity showed up that remains a passion to this day. Theatre! The school drama club held auditions for a production of *The Barretts of Wimpole Street*, so I ventured along. I was terrified, yet determined. To my surprise and delight, I got a role! As Wilson, the maid to Elizabeth Barrett, an English poet who was beloved of another poet, Robert Browning. I was beside myself with joy. I would go on stage! A more fitting and appropriate pursuit for me and my physical build than ballet!

Elizabeth Barrett was an invalid who had a cocker spaniel named Flush as her constant companion. The school's physical education teacher had a spaniel that she loaned to the production. I had to share several scenes with her. It was years later that I learned the important theatre adage "never share the stage with children or animals."

Center stage on the set that functioned as the family's living room was a large fireplace. While the set was being built, the dog joined rehearsals. She found an opening in the fireplace through which she would wander. On opening night, she decided to use that exit in the middle of a tense scene. I was holding her leash; it stretched as far as it would go until she disappeared, pulling me with her. I had no option but to go too, through the fireplace with my backside in the air, and the audience in hysterics. I was mortified. Had I ruined the production? Would the director ever forgive me? Was this the start, and end, of my theatrical career? It turned out to be the hit of the night, but the designer blocked the hole and it didn't happen again during the rest of the play's very short run.

Soon after that, the local Shirley Boys' High invited a few Avonside girls to join their school drama club for a couple of productions. I was included. I was over the moon! They'd noticed me! In one of the productions, I had to play a drunken middle-aged woman. In the other, I played the mother of Ned Kelly, an Australian outlaw. My body shape in those days was (and still is!) perfect for character and "motherly" roles.

These plays helped me to slowly ease into socializing with boys, something I'd been very self-conscious about. Vy and I went to parties together (I usually drove), and she would be mobbed. I was left alone. In the '60s it was customary for the host mum to provide a supper. I liked to help in the kitchen. I'd always stand behind sofas so that others would have to look at only half of me. Vy would be taken home by one of her adoring admirers. I'd drive myself home and cry myself to sleep.

Mum used to be concerned for me about the "boy" situation, but never gave me any helpful advice about dating or relationships. I guess because she'd been swept off her feet by Dad, she hadn't had to worry about being appealing. They'd met at his gym class in the small South Island town of Timaru. Mum told me, "Many of the girls in the class were very attractive, so I was surprised that Dad picked me."

She fell under his spell quickly and was excited to marry a man from a family with a respected "name" in Christchurch. My paternal grandfather was the highly regarded city pharmacist. Mum would leverage her status by marrying into a wealthier family than the one she'd grown up in. Sadly, she didn't heed the words of her own mother, who said to her, shortly before their wedding, "If you marry that man, you'll have a life of misery!" OMG, was she right!

Theatre was now a part of my life. I was overwhelmed when the senior boys at Shirley left school and formed a theatre troupe called The Group and invited me to join. They performed plays at a local café, and my parents agreed that I could participate. For three years (until I was nineteen) I rehearsed, romped, and ran raucously through the coffee house, reciting words from plays by Eugene Ionesco and Samuel Beckett, which I didn't really understand. I didn't really care. It was bliss.

During these years, the tension between my parents increased. At dinnertimes, when Dad deigned to dine with us, I continued to fight to swallow my food. I was in a heightened state of anxiety at home and felt panicky when alone with my father. Through my high school years, I experienced severe pain from my groin to my feet, which our family doctor couldn't diagnose. It wasn't cramps. Vy would come into the house and wait patiently until the pain had lifted enough for me to get on my bike. It always seemed strange to me that none of my classmates experienced the symptoms that debilitated me. Mum took me to the doctor, an old, expressionless soul. All he said was "Jennifer has growing pains; they'll go away eventually." Which they did ... eventually.

As money was always a troubling topic at home, my guilty nature made me believe I should start earning some. Much to my surprise, and that of my parents, I'd been accredited with the "University Entrance Certificate" that was based on my fourth year's exam results. It felt like a respectable juncture to step into the work world. I was sixteen and told my parents, "I want to leave school at the end of the year." They remonstrated a bit, but not heavily. Education wasn't their mainstay. I wish they'd made it mine. "If it feels right for you, you should do it," my father responded. He'd hated school.

Very quickly, I landed a job in administration at the registry office of the University of Canterbury, in Christchurch. This position required some work on the switchboard, responding to students at reception, and sorting exam papers and results. The latter role was a nightmare, as many of my friends attended the university; when they found out where I worked, they besieged me with bribes!

"Go on, Jen, just take a peek at my results. I won't tell anyone!"

"Not on your life!" I snapped back.

Happily, I never gave in.

I wish I'd completed a degree. I should have recognized the power that a university qualification would have afforded me. At the time I wasn't willing to put in the work. I bypassed an opportunity that would bug me until I reached my thirties, when a new opportunity for learning crossed my path.

CHAPTER 7

This above all; to thine own self be true.
Hamlet

A very special person in my life was my maternal grand-mother. I adored her. She was my solace during my teenage years. Nana lived a few blocks from my home, and every Wednesday after school, I'd bike to her place and stay the night. Ostensibly to keep her company, but in reality, an escape for me. "I've made trifle" (my favorite dessert), she'd say with a grin, as I pulled my bike up onto her porch. She'd wrap her plump arms around me and draw me into her large bosom for one of the best hugs in the world.

After dinner, we'd work on crossword puzzles. "That word was on the tip of my tongue," she would say as I answered yet another clue for her. We'd dance to songs on the radio, then I would go off to bed and sleep like a baby on a lumpy mattress. In the morning, she woke me with a cup of tea and some toast, and I'd bike off to school feeling refreshed and reinvigorated. And very loved.

On many occasions I met Nana at a movie theatre in town on a Friday night. She'd bring a bag of sandwiches for my dinner. The lights would go down and we'd immerse ourselves in the "film du jour." *The Sound of Music, The Song of Bernadette, The Inn of the Sixth Happiness, The King and I, Singin' in the Rain*—they were magical hours.

When I was nineteen, Nana developed angina (from coronary artery disease) and died in my arms. I hoped I would die too. I couldn't imagine life without her. I can remember going outside into the garden and looking up at the night sky, tears streaming down my face, and yelling at whoever was listening: "How dare you take her away!" To this day, I talk to her and seek her advice. She never fails me.

I threw myself into my job at the registry and had a lot of fun, especially when one of the girls I worked with started talking about her plans to travel to England! The "homeland" had always fascinated me for its history, pageantry, and theatre, so when she asked if I would go with her, I jumped at the opportunity. I started saving like mad.

I needed a second job. I approached the staff at the student cafeteria to see if they had any job openings. They did, and I was given the arduous task of washing all the pots, pans, plates, and cutlery used by a couple of hundred hungry, messy students. I would go home reeking of mashed potatoes and meat, my hands red and raw, but the dollars started mounting up in my bank account.

My father thought the trip would be important for me. My mother not so much. With her mother's death so recent, she couldn't bear the thought of "losing" me too. I knew I'd desperately miss my wonderful nieces and nephews; however, I forged ahead with planning and saving. In January 1970 I boarded the Chandris Lines' S.S. *Australis* and sailed into the wild blue yonder.

THIRD DECADE

1969–1979

GROWING

REFLECTIONS

This is a heck of a decade in which to grow. The world is your oyster, and you, the pearl. Fully formed and glistening. Awaiting the opening of your shell as you make your debut. A bit like Botticelli's *Venus*. So much lies ahead, and it's yours for the taking. Adventures, escapades, assignations. And just so you don't think it's all play, responsibilities too!

You're working now and earning money. Learning how to invest and grow your nest egg. Maybe that money you've earned is put toward travel so you can discover all the world has to offer. Maybe for a down payment on a home, a car, or a business.

You're making more decisions now. Do you want to live alone or with others? Are you in a relationship and want to move in with your partner? Or do you find there's so much to consider that your head's in a whirl? That's OK too. Your path is your destiny, so you lay the paving stones.

You might have already reached the place you want to be for the rest of your life, in a secure job, with secure remuneration, and a bright future. Great! But do ask yourself this: Will my fifty-year-old self be happy with where I am right now? Or does she want me to do something new and different? Take risks?

Be kind to yourself. Bite off large chunks of life and chew them well. Run, walk, swim, play, sit, read, relax, cook, travel. These are some of the best years of your life! You won't get them back. Grow into them!

CHAPTER 8

To unpathed waters, undreamed shores.
The Winter's Tale

The ship, *Australis*, of the Chandris Lines (formerly a US Navy troopship during WWII and an immigrant ship from England to Australia) sailed from the New Zealand port of Auckland. It looked enormous as I stood on the wharf with my shabby suitcases, waiting to board. What the hell was I doing? Could I really live on this giant tub for the next five weeks? Could I handle whatever was waiting at the other end? Yes, I could! It was the ticket I'd been waiting for. My ticket to freedom!

Vy and James came to say goodbye. When they visited my cabin, they marveled at how many things fitted into such a small space. Bunk beds, tiny sets of drawers, and a minuscule shower. There were many tears as I farewelled my friends from the top of the gangway.

I'll never forget the moment the ship cast off and we slowly and majestically moved away from the wharf. Thousands of streamers (mostly toilet paper) filled the air, and thousands of tears streamed down our cheeks. As the last tie broke, we slipped the bountiful bonds of Aotearoa and journeyed to foreign climes, the strains of the gorgeous song "Po Atarau" ("Now is the Hour") fading into the distance.

There were four of us in our tiny berth on the third deck, with no porthole. The other three were girls I hadn't met before. One remains a friend to this day. The work associate who'd persuaded me to take the trip with her left her booking late and ended up in an awful cabin near the engine room. We all headed to the deck frequently to view the magnificent ocean vista and escape the confines of our cramped cabins. God, how I loved it when the whitecaps on the waves soared so high that the foam hit us in the face. There was nothing but the Tasman Sea between New Zealand and Australia, and our first stop, Sydney!

I had ventured to Oz when I was eighteen and spent a couple of days in Sydney; however, this visit felt deliciously different. The Harbor Bridge and the Opera House stood grandly beside us as we pulled into Port Botany. We scrambled all over The Rocks (the historical network of lanes and alleys beside the harbor), peering into shop windows, tasting some of the local food, and listening to the buskers on the seafront.

Next stop, Fiji, and brand-new territory. I loved the sultry heat and the friendly people but hated the kava kava (an intoxicating pepper drug) we tried to swallow at a welcome ceremony for the ship. It's considered impolite to refuse the gritty substance, but the rebel in me spat it out.

Acapulco was our destination many days later. A completely different world. The immense wealth juxtaposed to abject poverty hit my senses immediately. We spent a fascinating day exploring the back streets of the city, while some from the ship preferred to sit by the ocean drinking exotic cocktails. I bought crudely made puppets from a street vendor to send home to my nieces and nephews.

The trip through the 80 km Panama Canal was fascinating. Opened in 1914, the first year of the Great War, this more than eleven-hour passage connects the Pacific and Atlantic Oceans. Watching the sides of our giant ship sink lower and lower into the water as the canal sides rose higher and higher underscored the engineering wonder. I marveled that we didn't get stuck, as the space between the ship and the canal walls was hardly visible.

Reaching the Atlantic was a sizable shock for the senses! It was as if the mighty ocean knew that its duty was to rise and fall like a giant monster, crashing as it dipped and tipping as it rose. The captain warned us of the change that was coming and advised those who experienced seasickness to take to their beds and stay there while we plunged through the waves for several days. I have to admit, I loved it!! Wrapped up in warm, waterproof clothing, I walked the deck inhaling the bracing sea air while fighting the pitching and whorling. I saw only one other passenger doing the same. Perhaps we were both nuts, but hey, we didn't care!

Our last stop before England was Miami, Florida. It was my first encounter with America, and I wasn't overly impressed. The area near the port was seedy, and a group of us were quite shocked when we peered through the windows of a porn shop.

The guys thought it was great! There were things in that store that fitted human body parts in ways I didn't recognize and couldn't imagine.

Our departure from Miami was different from any of our other port departures because two of my cabinmates missed it! They got waylaid in a bar with some local guys and lost track of time. We'd set sail by the time they got to the wharf. I was in a lather, but there was nothing I could do. One of them got extremely upset on the dock and wailed and gnashed her teeth; the other sat down on a bollard and started writing a postcard to her parents: "Dear Mum and Dad, the *Australis* looks great from where I'm sitting in Miami, as it heads out to sea …" She had to phone her parents, and heaven knows what dear Mum and Dad had to pay for the ship to turn around and return to the dock to pick them up. They were the topic of much gossip for days.

Life on board the *Australis* was a constant party. We danced with the crew to *Zorba the Greek* and boogied our buns off to the hits of the '70s. A large percentage of the passengers were young like me; we'd saved our money to go on the high seas for our big "OE" (Overseas Experience). People had suggested I fly to London, but I didn't want to. As I'd not been away from home for an extended period before, I wanted to transition slowly into this new world.

The partying was more subdued in the last few days of the five-week journey; however, we made the most of it, relishing flirtations, clandestine meetings, and (mostly) good food, knowing it would all end soon.

We steamed into Southampton and into a pea soup fog, the likes of which I'd never seen. It was unnerving arriving in a strange land not being able to see even an outline of a building. We scrambled our bags together, ready to disembark from our sea home. We took a train from Southampton to Waterloo Station in London, then hailed a cab to take us to our digs (a bed-and-breakfast we'd booked from New Zealand). We didn't see much on the way to Waterloo; however, the fog had lifted in London and the sights were visible.

I'll never forget the lovely cabbie who, upon learning that it was our first trip to England, took us on a magical tour beside the River Thames, past the Houses of Parliament and Big Ben, round the Tower of London and across Tower Bridge, all for the regular fare! It was a glorious introduction that had me shedding tears of joy.

CHAPTER 9

What is the city but the people?
Coriolanus

We were 18,695 km (11,616 miles) from home, and so far, so good. We were finding our feet on the pavements of London. But we had to learn to navigate the Underground! The Tube, as it's affectionately known, has a map that's a beginner's nightmare. (Thanks *are* due to Harry Beck, a 29-year-old electrical draftsman, who in 1931 designed and sketched the original.) With the map color-coded, complex, and confusing to an "immigrant," we took many a journey in the wrong direction, sheepishly alighting to cross the station and catch the right train.

Next stop, New Zealand House, in the heart of Piccadilly, where we'd been told we would find accommodation and a job. The place was abuzz with young folks from our native land. Scanning through dozens of notes pinned to a board, we found a flat in North London that sounded excellent that was "looking for two girls to join." I picked up a couple of secretarial job offerings that sounded appealing. Life in London was underway!

We "interviewed" at the flat in Canfield Gardens and were accepted into the fold. The house had three floors, and our space was on the top. It slept five. However, after a few months there, our numbers had swelled to nine. More expats from New Zealand arrived. Fortunately, four of the roomies were night nurses, so when they came home in the early morning, they got into the beds that those of us with day jobs had just vacated. We were never sure if we slept in very clean or very dirty sheets!

I wrote the first of hundreds of letters home. I've read those letters in recent years, and the excitement falls off each page filled with wondrous discoveries and amazing sights. I felt I had to write frequently to keep Mum going. There were some days I felt very tired, but I wrote anyway, out of guilt about being so far away.

I landed my first job—as a secretary at the Middle Temple between Fleet Street and the River Thames (the headquarters of the Knights Templar, who fought in the Crusades, until they were dissolved in 1312). The Temple is part of the Inns of Court, populated by barristers who prosecute and defend at the Royal Courts of Justice and the Old Bailey. It was like stepping back in time in old London. The QC (Queen's Counsel) who was head of Chambers interviewed me. Seated in a wing-backed chair wearing a three-piece suit, with his superb British accent, he was intimidating. I felt like Eliza Doolittle. I sounded like her too. In fact, when the barristers gathered to have tea in the mornings in my reception area, they would ask, "Jen, say 'six,' 'no,' 'yes,' and 'thank you.' We love your strange Kiwi vowel pronunciations!" Gradually, their English accents rubbed off on me, and when I returned to New Zealand three years later, I sounded almost as upper class as they did.

I worked hard, saved hard, and played hard. We had some great pubs in our area, and many a night was spent in Ye Olde Swiss Cottage, swilling cider. After six months, four of us from the flat set off on our first tour of Europe—the first of many forays into the incredible world of new cultures, monuments, art galleries, museums, cathedrals, exciting food, interesting young men, and some wild nightlife.

Every penny I could spare was spent on theatre tickets. I scoured the newspaper and selected the show I had to see and often lined up for an hour or more to get a cheap ticket. I stood transfixed for three and a half hours in the nose-bleed section of the Royal Opera House when New Zealand's Dame Kiri Te Kanawa sang the role of Susanna in *The Marriage of Figaro*. I attended Moliere's *The Imaginary Invalid* at the National Theatre. Just before curtain-up, the lead actor, Edward Petherbridge, stepped downstage to announce that Sir Laurence Olivier had died. A little bit of me died too, and after the performance, I wandered around the theatre lobby to soak up his memory.

All the while, I wrote home profusely, sharing every adventure (well, nearly every) and reveled in the news I got about the family—especially the children, who I missed terribly. I was envious when my flatmates talked lovingly about their fathers. I couldn't talk about mine that way. To this day, I envy my friends who have or had great dads.

We ate an awful lot of bread during those first months. It added pounds to my already overweight body. The winter was bleak, the flat cold, the bread cheap, and there was a postal strike in Britain, so we didn't get any letters from home.

The next three years were a tapestry of travel, toil, and testing. And love. Overall, I traveled about 80,000 km through Europe and the Scandinavian countries, with different groups of friends each time. We "camped" in Norway in the middle of winter, four of us huddled on a toilet block floor, wrapped in our tent. We slept under canvas beside the Loire River, and when it flooded, the water streamed through our tent. We were "picked up" by a group of Italian men outside Amalfi. They noticed that one of the tires on our vehicle was flat and took us back to their house for three days while it was mended! We danced on tables in Austrian heurigers, had leather pantsuits made in the market in Istanbul, and danced in the streets of Dubrovnik. A beautiful Greek man fell "in love" with me, and despite my remonstrations, turned up unexpectedly on my doorstep in London. That was one for the books, as I'd never really been noticed before.

Back in London, the toil took over as I worked to save for the next trip. I was lucky enough to get a Christmas holiday job at Harrods, the iconic department store. It was for six weeks only. We were told to wear black or gray dresses and taught how to walk around the department with our hands firmly clasped behind our backs. I was assigned to the gift department and served some interesting people. Comedian John Cleese, actress Glenda Jackson, the Duke of Kent, and one day, Princess Anne shopped in our little corner.

The biggest thrill was selling a gorgeous Spanish wooden chess set to actor Richard Harris, whom I idolized. When he first approached me in the store, I didn't realize it was him, with his sunglasses and hat over his eyes, although his mellifluous voice nearly knocked me over. My associates told me who he was after he left. The next day he returned, and I was away at my mandatory tea break. When I returned to the department, he came rushing over. I fell to pieces and could hardly speak, I was so overcome. "I wanted to purchase the set from you, in case you get commission," he said, to a pathetic "thank you" from me. If this scene were repeated today, I'd offer to personally deliver the pieces to his home.

I met actor Roger Moore ("James Bond") while I was working in a child-minding job. My flatmates were furious that I didn't invite him home with me! I was looking after two obnoxious children who lived with their mother in Harley Street, in central London, which has been noted since the nineteenth century for its large number of private specialists in surgery and medicine. She told me that the milkman would deliver and expect to be paid, and "Do *not* let the children out when you open the door!"

Minutes after she left, the little boy stuffed all the bed pillows down the toilets! Then the milkman arrived. I put the door on a latch, but the boy undid it in a flash and shot out the door, followed by his sister, and up the nearby staircase. I jammed the door open and tore up the stairs to hear the most gorgeous voice say, "Are you looking for *these*?" Moore was standing a few stairs up from me, with a child under each arm. I was puffing, red in the face, and furious. "Yes, I am, thank you," I stammered, staring into his vivid blue eyes. With huge embarrassment, I grabbed each child by the hand and dragged them back to their home.

Sir William and Lady Norah Ramsay unexpectedly became dear friends. Sir William (or Bill, as he became known to me) was the president of the English Rugby Board. I was introduced to him by one of my uncles who had held the similar position in New Zealand. Uncle Tom wrote to Bill to tell him I was coming to London and asked, "Would you please keep an eye on Jennifer in case she needs money or runs off the rails?" Such confidence in me!

Bill, Norah, and I became very good friends. Once a month, on a Sunday, they invited me to their home in Belgravia for a luncheon. Looking back, those were some of the richest days of my life. Unfortunately, I had little understanding of the wealth of knowledge and experience seated at their table. Edward Heath was the prime minister at the time. Lords and Ladies, ministers of defense, sport, law, commerce and more shared lively conversation and multiple insights into the government. I could have learned so much if only I'd listened and taken notice!

CHAPTER 10

I would not wish any companion in the world but you.
The Tempest

Learning to manage my finances and resources in a new country was often "hard yakka" (a Kiwi expression for hard work)! While there were plenty of highs, there were also lots of lows. Not everything came up roses. Working long days, getting up in the dark in a London winter, taking three trains to work for some jobs, getting home in the dark to a cold flat and a meal of steamed cabbage and a poached egg (money was tight), drying my one pair of stockings under the stove grill (praying they wouldn't catch fire), and sleeping in a lumpy bed in a room with others was not the life of a princess.

But it taught me a lot about resilience, personal strength, and independence. I'm not saying that I had all three completely sussed. However, those years in London brought out a side of myself that I hadn't recognized before. I realized I could handle just about anything.

Resilience is an interesting word. Psychologists define resilience as "the process of adapting well in the face of adversity, trauma, tragedy, threats, or significant sources of stress—such as family and relationship problems, serious health problems, or workplace and financial stressors." I guess I'd experienced a few of those!

I'd left New Zealand with a lot of pain in my heart. The more I focused on the new tasks at hand, the better I felt. I realized that an occupied mind and body can lead to healthier thoughts and actions. We can all fall prey to negativity. One of the songs from Monty Python's movie *The Life of Brian* gives good advice: "Always look on the bright side of life" (da dum, da dum, da dumdadumdadum … you know you know it)! On days that are tough and relentless, it can feel impossible to be positive. However, when thoughts are turned toward the bright side, the day can change.

We're all born with differing types of strength. Watch a baby try to cross a room, a child mastering an important skill, a disabled person negotiating a difficult doorway. Each has a specific strength that comes from within. An essence. Nowadays, when I look in the mirror, I look for strength rather than flaws. I hold my head higher, pull my back straighter, plant my feet firmly, square my shoulders, and smile. My loins are girded.

I mentioned my independence. Ostensibly the word means freedom, clear of constraints, especially from others. Independence has us working separately, with a sense of self-control and autonomy. Independence can create self-esteem and self-value. "I'm here on this earth with a purpose, and I'm purposeful!" I was beginning to matter to myself.

Another cliff I had to climb was learning to live with others from differing backgrounds and cultures. While mostly exhilarating, some didn't care about a clean house and were happy to leave the cleaning to the rest of us; others didn't have money for the rent and assumed we would cover for them; a few brought their boyfriends home and had sex with them in the big, shared bedroom, while we hung around outside, waiting to go to bed!

What about boyfriends for me? Well, in my third year in London, 1973, I had a second job, working as a barmaid in the Angel and Crown pub in Richmond. (I was living in a flat near Kew Gardens at the time.) A Chilean man named Leo came into the pub occasionally, and he and I struck up conversations. One evening, he was still there at closing. "May I drive you home?" That was the beginning of a beautiful yearlong relationship that concluded with a proposal of marriage and the offer of a life in Valparaiso, Chile. However, I had made the decision (through my guilt) to return to New Zealand at the end of that year. My flights were booked. Despite loving him, I felt I had to go home.

I'll always remember the teary day we had to say our farewells. We'd reached a compromise. I would fly home, we would stay closely in touch, and I would eventually meet him in Chile, and we'd marry.

The marriage never came to pass. I landed back in Christchurch a much-changed young woman. My nieces and nephews ran out onto the tarmac when my plane landed (something they'd never do today)! It was beyond thrilling to wrap my arms around them for the first time in three years. My parents were overwhelmed to have me back, but their feelings were not reciprocated. After all the freedom I'd experienced, I felt imprisoned and trapped at home. And that same dark undercurrent still pervaded the house.

I wrote to Leo daily, and we talked by phone. As the weeks wore on, I realized that I wasn't going to travel to Chile and broke the news to him in a 22-page letter. He was devastated, as was I, but it was best to face the truth. We stayed in touch for months afterwards, and I remember him with great fondness. I hope wherever he is, he's happy.

CHAPTER 11

The labor we delight in physics pain.
Macbeth

Three months after returning home to New Zealand, I moved into a large house owned by a couple of friends. I visited Mum and Dad frequently. Mum especially wanted to lean on me again, but I had to retain my freedom and independence.

It was time to find work! I'd been living off funds remaining from my time in London (scarce though they were). Besides, I needed to be fully occupied. The 1974 Commonwealth Games were held in Christchurch, and I got a job as secretary to the press editor. It was for only five weeks and was interesting and frantic. Before the games started, we set up machines and equipment to be ready for the news feeds to and from the world.

Queen Elizabeth II opened the games. The Duke of Edinburgh accompanied her. We watched their loo being built in the corridor along from our office. It was off-limits, of course. Those of us with the devil in us took a look inside but stopped short of actually peeing in the royal pot!

The games were very exciting, with athletes from all the Commonwealth countries participating. At times it was chaos in the press room—reporters don't do things quietly—but exhilarating. When the games ended, the editor offered me a job in Wellington, the nation's capital city, as his assistant. I turned it down. Out of guilt. I couldn't leave Christchurch *again*.

God, I hate guilt! It's an insidious creature. It pervades the mind by throwing in all sorts of comments, thoughts, and rules that alter thinking patterns. Some people unknowingly trigger guilt. Others create it deliberately with messages like "You should ..." "I thought you were going to ..." "Didn't you say you were ...?" and many more versions.

I've carried guilt for much of my life. Life is hard enough; none of us should be bogged down by debilitating messages in our brains. I've missed some great opportunities because of guilt about not being good enough, smart enough, or worthy enough. Nowadays we call that "impostor syndrome," a distasteful idiom.

It was time to find a real job. A brand-new computer company in Christchurch was looking for a personal assistant for the two founders of the company and two senior executives. The interview with one of the founders was great fun. When he learned that I'd just spent three years in London—one of his favorite cities—he asked me copious questions about my experiences. At the end of the interview, he inquired somewhat sheepishly: "You do have shorthand and typing skills, don't you?"

I stayed in that fabulous job for nine years. The senior founder, Bernard, was like a father to me—the father I'd never had. Caring, solicitous, and so, so intelligent. He was on the boards of numerous leading New Zealand companies and highly respected in the business world. The day he died was one of the saddest days of my life.

All the men treated me so well that I began to realize my personal value. I was wined and dined, expanded my skillset, and met some wonderful business leaders. I planned the company's conferences, went sailing with Bernard, and was mentored and encouraged by all my bosses. I was twenty-four, yet still very insecure internally. They saw this and boosted my self-esteem. Bernard said to me one day, "You know you could do anything you put your mind to, don't you?" I was overwhelmed. He had opened a chink in my persona that began to grow hope and optimism.

The only thing I couldn't overcome in my time working with them was wage equity! Whenever I asked for a raise (when it was due and others in the company were getting theirs), I was turned down. I worked hard and wanted to put more money into savings. They insisted, "Jenni, you're treated very well; you get a lot of perks and you're paid pretty well." Today, I would say, "Bullshit!"

The gender pay gap is one of my pet peeves. One study (Center for American Progress) found that women on average could be paid nearly a *half million dollars less* than their male counterparts over the course of a forty-year career. Women of color, LGBTQ women, and women with other identities are held back at even greater disadvantages. Today, many companies are addressing this issue, but women still have a long way to go to reach full equity.

CHAPTER 12

Love sought is good, but given unsought is better.
Twelfth Night

It was time to reignite my love of theatre! I joined a local amateur company and performed in five plays in one year. The theatrical world helped me retain the magic that London had provided, and shined a light in the darkness I still felt from my familial home. I visited frequently and was happiest when Mum and I could chat while my father was shut away in his shed.

An interesting opportunity showed up through new friends. They suggested that I might like to train as a communications specialist with the New Zealand Marriage Guidance Council in Christchurch. Now, I thought, I'm approaching thirty, unmarried, so what use would I be? Well, as it turned out, I was accepted and spent two years studying with the council while learning significant interpersonal communication skills.

A favorite activity was spending an evening with about fifty young men at a local detention center to discuss their needs. They weren't hardened criminals; they'd gone astray because they didn't have positive role models at home. So I developed role plays of their family situations. Often I acted as one of them while they portrayed a parent. I'd kick furniture, mumble incoherently, talk back and use foul language. The young man playing my parent would admonish me or tell me to "tone it down." We'd all discuss the scenario and they began to understand the power of constructive communication. I learned a lot from those young men and hope they found a better path in life.

I dated occasionally, but none of the relationships went anywhere. At one stage, I was going out with three guys! They were all platonic relationships and very different men. I played squash with one of them, and we threw dinner parties at his lovely flat. I think he was gay. Another was a recently divorced architect and poet who would call me in the middle of the night to read some pathetic verse he'd written about unrequited love. The third was a delightful young man, eight years younger than me. He and I walked on the beach a lot and made out in the dunes. I turned thirty while we were dating. To mark the occasion, he bought me thirty carnations. I think he got such a hell of a shock at how many flowers there were that my birthday date was our last!

The stigma around older women dating younger men still exists. I must admit, however, I do like the term "cougar"! Why does it seem to be OK for older men to date younger women? Very sexist in my opinion. If you're in a relationship with a younger person that feels right and you have more in common than sex, go for it! Age is only a number; and it's the age of your heart that counts.

One of the executives at the computer company who had never dated as far as we knew surprised and delighted us all one morning by telling us he'd become engaged. It turned out that his fiancée was living in a one-bedroom apartment beside the Avon River in Christchurch and would be leaving it to move into their marital home. "Would you be interested in seeing it, Jenni, and perhaps renting it?" Would I ever! And so it was that I moved into a darling little flat, where I could flaunt my privacy and be me entirely.

My nieces and nephews were at various stages at boarding school. We had such fun when I picked them up on Sundays to spend the day at my flat. We would cook, play music, and talk about life while they sat on my little balcony and smoked (not permitted, but hey, their parents weren't around). I took them back to the boarding house with tins filled with cake and goodies.

Life in my hometown was settling into a comfortable routine. And as 1979 ended and a new decade began, life was about to change dramatically!

Fourth Decade

1979–1989

Loving

REFLECTIONS

Aah, the thirties! This is a decade most people look back on and smile. So much gets defined here. Who you are and what you want. Your professional role is established, and possibly your relationship with a partner is too. Or maybe partnering's just not for you and you prefer to paddle your own canoe. You might be a parent. That could mean you're juggling home life with your work life.

People are recognizing you for your skills and attributes. Promotions are strong possibilities. Financially, you're stable, or at least getting there. Maybe you own property and you've set up a nest you can call your own. Oh boy, that means there's a mortgage to pay and repairs to be done. But life is productive and vigorous.

It's a great time to try new things. Dance like no one's watching, jump out of a plane, hike the Inca Trail; you get the picture. It's a great way to further develop your own identity. Shape your own mold. Be the "who" you are meant to be.

You're probably taking better care of your body. You realize it doesn't have an unlimited lifetime guarantee! Sadly, flaws in your physiology will start to show up. Be prepared for these. And don't ignore them!

Probably your parents or guardians are ageing. There's another responsibility to shoulder. *"The wheel is come full circle."* Those who cared for us now need caregiving.

And you still have a hunger to learn. To feel the vibrations of life. To be involved and participating on our planet. Never lose that zest for life, no matter what dark matter crosses your threshold.

CHAPTER 13

Is it possible that love should of a sudden take such a hold?
The Taming of the Shrew

Craig was a young male employee at the computer company in Christchurch who was a natural comedian. He was excellent at his IT work, while keeping us in stitches with his antics. He was invited by my bosses to open a company office in Sydney. Thrilling for him, but very sad for all of us, as we'd lose his personality from our midst.

When he sold his car before leaving for Australia, he asked one of his roommates, Kim, if he would drive him around Christchurch to say goodbye to close friends. They came to visit me on a Saturday morning, when I was head down and bum up cleaning the toilet. I was a mess, and so was the flat!

The only drink I had to toast him with was sherry. I poured some into pottery cups with chunks of ice and a sprig of mint (a very nice aperitif, as it turned out), and we drank to his future. All the while, Kim sat quietly in a corner, tugging at his beard, offering pithy comments from time to time.

The company threw a big farewell party for Craig. On the dance floor, I remember crashing into Kim, who was there with the girl he was dating. "Very sorry," I said. "Oh, nice to see you again," Kim replied, and that was that.

The following week I rang Craig's fiancée to see how she was doing. She was delighted to meet for a glass of wine at a very popular local bar. We enjoyed a marvelous conversation, then realized we were hungry. Just as we were getting up to leave, Kim walked in with another of his roommates. They'd come for a nightcap. When we told them we were heading out to eat, they walked with us to a nearby restaurant. I remember lively banter and lots of laughter.

"Why don't you come back to my place," I suggested, "and we could phone Craig?" "Great idea!" they echoed. So, we huddled up in my small space and called several times, with no answer. "Where is he?" his fiancée lamented. "He doesn't know anyone in Sydney." "That won't stop him from socializing," we all agreed. We gave up on the calls and talked until the small hours. Kim came out of his shell, and I enjoyed his great sense of humor.

The following Friday, my boss, Bernard, asked if I would look after Ed, a visiting American engineer who'd been working at the company all week. Bernard gave me the company credit card to use for all expenses. Wowee, what we could do with that! My older niece was working in Christchurch by this time, so I called her and asked her to join us. "Yes, please," came the enthusiastic reply. She was at my front door in minutes.

Just as we were about to leave and pick up Ed from his hotel, there was a knock on the door. It was Kim, with the same roommate from the previous week. "We just wanted to stop by and tell you the name of the movie we couldn't remember last Friday," was the excuse. "Oh, and take you out for a drink if you're free?" To this day, I don't remember discussing a movie!

A coup! Two nerdy blokes to entertain the visitor. Perfecto! Kim was researching his PhD in Respiratory Physiology at Princess Margaret Hospital in Christchurch, and his roomie was an engineer. Off we went to the hotel, then to a great bar. Sparks flew as the booze flowed. My niece fell in love with the engineer. I had to play the stern auntie and nip that in the bud. Then we all collapsed at my flat again for conversation past midnight. By now, Kim had memorized my phone number. (Those were the days of dial phones; does anyone remember *them*?)

During this period in 1980, there was a worldwide gas (petrol) shortage. As a consequence, New Zealanders had been asked to have one carless day per week. Mine was Wednesday. Kim knew this, and the following week, arrived at my front door.

"Just wondering if there's anything you need or anywhere you want to go, as I know you can't use your car today."

"I had planned to walk along the river to the museum, where they're showing an Italian movie, *Padre Padrone*."

"I like European movies. I'm happy to drive you there."

The lights went out and the movie began. Set in the hills of Italy on a farm, a young shepherd boy was tending the sheep. The next thing on screen was a close-up of the face of the boy and a lot of grunting. I realized with shock what was going on (the sheep probably had by then as well). "Bloody hell," I thought. "What's Kim going to think I am? Some kind of pervert?" I was glad it was dark. When the lights came up, I didn't look at Kim, but on the way home, I said, "Sorry about that, not quite what I was expecting!" "Neither was I," he replied. "But it gave me a very different impression of you and your predilections!" We both had a good laugh.

The following week, John, the emotional architect/poet who used to phone me in the middle of the night, came over for dinner at my flat. Halfway through our meal, there was a knock on the door. It was Kim with a bag of tomatoes from the garden at his flat. "We've got more of these than we can eat, thought you might like some." Candy and flowers are the usual wooing ploy; tomatoes were a new look.

I invited him in, and he sat comfortably with John and me and enjoyed a glass of wine. When he left, John said to me very slowly and carefully, "Don't let Kim think that there is anything between us, because that young man is in love with you."

"Excuse me?" I said. "In love with me? You've got to be kidding! He hardly knows me! What on earth would make you say that?"

"Because of the way he looks at you and talks to you," came John's reply.

I suddenly felt very hot and sweaty. Not with lust, but with overwhelming feelings. It had never occurred to me. I didn't have any feelings for Kim, or did I …?

CHAPTER 14

I love you with so much of my heart that none is left to protest.
Much Ado About Nothing

Abig debutante ball was coming up for one of Kim's friends. Kim had a partner; however, his engineer roommate didn't. Kim called me.

"Would you mind going to the ball with him?"

"No, I'm sorry. I'm not available."

He called again. "Are you sure I can't persuade you to go?"

I refused again. "I have nothing to wear to a ball!"

At 5 p.m. on the day of the ball, Kim made his final call.

"He'll be at your door in an hour!"

Bugger that, I thought! *Who do they think they are!*

In rebellion, I didn't shower and reluctantly put on my prettiest dress, stuck a flower in my hair and met the roommate at the door. It was a swanky "do," but great fun. During the evening, Kim's partner flitted off with her girlfriends. He and

I sat together and chatted. He looked very dapper in black tie. "Would you like to dance," he asked. He was shaking like a leaf, and I wasn't sure why! But I did feel good standing close to him.

A couple of weeks later, one of Kim's friends was having a farewell dinner before he left for his "OE" in England.

"Would you like to go?" Kim phoned and asked. "I'll pick you up and take you to the restaurant." I refused at first. Who would I know there? But he persuaded me.

When we walked into the restaurant, one of his former roommates was already sitting at our table with her husband. She leaned over to whisper something to him as we sat down. My culpable brain's first thought was that she said, "This woman's a lot older than Kim." I learned years later that what she said was, "Kim just walked in with his wife." That was our first "official" date. Kim had just come out of a more than three-year relationship. I had no thoughts of pinning him down.

Later that evening, we all went back to Kim's house for a party in his large bedroom. He had a great stereo system and we rocked the rafters. Kim had attended a private boys' school in his junior years and was very used to wearing a tie. Many of his friends knew this, so they opened his closet and brought out all the ties he had and put them on. Heaven only knows why, but it added to the fun!

I didn't have a tie, so Kim came up behind me and tied one around my neck. "Here, you should have one too." The vibes I got from his body, and mine, were electric. It was deliciously terrifying. So much so, I left soon after. This was too much to handle. However, I had learned one useful fact during the evening. The girl he was "dating" was gay and was only interested in Kim for friendship. Why was that such a relief?

He continued to call, and one day I bit the bullet and invited him over for dinner. He'd been very kind to me, so this would repay him. "I'd love to come, thanks!" It was the Friday of an Easter weekend. My neighbor across the landing lived alone, so I had invited her to come over for a sherry. She so enjoyed our company that she stayed forever, until dinner was ruined! But that was the first night Kim kissed me, and my appetite for food disappeared! Wow, he was hot!

For the next three weeks we dated solidly, catching every available moment to be alone. We never left each other on the weekends. We drove regularly to a nearby town called Hanmer where there was a lovely forest area called Conical Hill. We learned about each other as we walked up and down under the pines.

One night, we crashed into bed after downing a few brandies. Suddenly, he said, "I can't breathe."

I leapt up and turned on the light. "What can I do? Open the window, get you water …?"

"No, I'll be OK. I think I know what's happening."

He was out of bed by this time, looked me in the eyes, and said, "Will you marry me?"

OMG, now *I* felt faint. After all my years of deciding I'd probably stay single, here was a proposal of marriage from a man I'd only just met.

"Yes!" I squealed.

He was 23 and I was 31, and it didn't matter. It was bliss!

We decided not to tell anyone about being "secretly" engaged. Kim was concerned. "I don't have anything to offer you at this stage in the way of job stability until I finish my PhD."

That was unimportant to me. What I had found in him was brilliance, stability, kindness, caring, and integrity—all the things lacking in my father.

Without realizing it, I'd found a partner with attributes that were the antithesis of the man who had fathered me. Over the years, friends have asked me, "How did you know so soon that you wanted to marry Kim? I've been dating the same person for months/years now and I'm still not sure."

My questions in return: "Do they treat you with respect? Do they respect themselves? Are they kind to you? What's their relationship like with their parents and friends? Do you always feel safe when you're with them? Can you see a future with them?"

Kim ticked all these boxes. And another benefit I could add? It's OK to choose a younger partner. They're like puppies—you can train them!

CHAPTER 15

Self-love is not so vile a sin as self-neglecting.
Henry V

A few weeks into our relationship, Kim arrived early at my flat and I wasn't dressed to go out yet. I went overboard with apologies. He said, "Do you realize how many times you say, 'I'm sorry?' You've only got to apologize for living and you will have covered the whole gamut. You have nothing to apologize for."

What a wake-up call. I hadn't realized how much my low self-esteem showed up. Over time, even though the tendency remained, I changed "sorry" to "I apologize" because it sounded sexier and much more mature, and then I dropped it altogether (unless, of course, I do some real damage to someone).

When I run training programs for women, I constantly hear the words "I'm sorry ..." before a woman states her thoughts; before she makes a presentation; when she makes a mistake;

when she feels she is holding up the pace of the program. On and on it goes. I take the time to go over *my* lesson with all the women in the room and stress the importance of not apologizing for oneself. We have no need to. We are strong and resilient. We hold up half the sky. We don't owe apologies. We owe our words, opinions, and actions to the world. Deliver them unapologetically!

Kim and I told our parents of our engagement. They were very happy. I approached Kim's parents alone for a few moments and asked how they felt about my being eight years older than Kim. Kim's dad's reply: "Our only problem would be if you *weren't* marrying him!" That brought a grateful tear to my eye.

When I told Bernard, he leapt from behind his desk, threw his arms around me, congratulated me, and then said, "I'll lose you now." I was confused. Getting engaged didn't mean leaving my job; we weren't living in the 1800s. "Kim will get a position overseas when he's completed his PhD," he said. What a prophecy that turned out to be!

On the day we announced our engagement in the newspaper (taking all our friends by surprise), the phone started ringing at my flat. Kim leapt out of bed and rushed off to work without breakfast. The Court Theatre was staging a lunchtime fashion show, of which I was the emcee. I saw Kim at the theatre, where lunch was finger sandwiches and sherry, and lots of congratulations. That evening my company threw me a party, which meant more drinks and very little food for Kim. When we eventually returned to my flat, he spent our first, enchanted, engaged evening throwing up in the toilet.

After the fashion show, the modeling agent had approached me and asked if I would consider being trained as a model at their studios! I felt faint. Me, a model, with my low self-esteem and "body-shaming" mindset.

"She'll call you on Monday," came a voice from my left. Kim, of course, encouraging me to step outside myself into a world that hadn't even been a dream, but that would fill my life for two years. I learned so much, wore some gorgeous clothes, and grew "inches" in my own esteem. I loved modeling garments for larger women, as they could see themselves in the outfits I wore.

Nowadays we're urged to call the women in our lives "strong, clever, intelligent, and smart" rather than "pretty, sweet, or gorgeous" as I was by my father. I wish I'd been encouraged to look at photos of women who achieved great things in their lives and who also happened to be abundantly curvaceous. I might have seen myself there, and I'm sure it would have made me stronger.

Former Georgia Representative Stacey Abrams is a perfect example! Brilliant, strong, opinionated, and Black, she's a role model for women. Taylor Swift and Lady Gaga are two more examples. They don't think of themselves as attractive; they prefer intelligent. And the inimitable actor Dame Judi Dench (who I have met!) referred to herself as a "menopausal dwarf," then graced the cover of *Vogue*!

CHAPTER 16

Now join your hands, and with your hands your hearts.
Henry VI, Part 3

Kim and I embarked on wedding plans, including our parents every step of the way. Kim came fabric-shopping with me (to the surprise of my girlfriends) and helped me choose the material for my dress and those of the bridesmaids—my two nieces. At the store, two beautiful fabrics were on display. "There's your dress, and the girls' dresses," Kim said. I loved them both, but needed him to know that women don't choose anything that quickly when shopping. We must look at everything! Which we did. Guess which fabrics we bought?

The dressmaking books featured wedding dresses that were too fluffy and fussy for me. I asked a close family friend if she would design my dress. Vy Elsom was a noted New Zealand artist (she had painted Queen Elizabeth II), so I was honored that she agreed. We sat in her lounge, she with two pieces of white card and black pen, me with a head full of ideas. After an hour, she turned the cards toward me and there was my gown, front and back, exactly as I had imagined! Another close friend cut out the pattern and made my dress, which I have to this day (though fit me it doesn't). The dress and veil cost me $200.00.

Although it's none of my business, I'm always shocked when I hear the prices some brides pay for their wedding outfits. A deposit on a car could be paid for the cost of a dress!

February 6, 1982, our wedding day, dawned sunny and warm. I was staying at my parents' home (following the old-fashioned custom of not seeing my groom after midnight). The usual tense undercurrent had lifted temporarily because of the happy occasion. Anyway, my head was filled with starting a new life with a wonderful partner, and Dad couldn't spoil that.

Dad was a highly emotional man, and when we reached the church door, before proceeding up the long aisle, he started breathing very deeply and noisily. "I don't want to cry and upset your day," he said. Well, that didn't work. Kim heard us before he saw us!

We had a fabulous day, great food, wonderful people, and danced into the evening. A friend sang Cole Porter's "Begin the Beguine" for our first dance, which we fumbled through with lots of giggling.

We invited all our friends and family who had traveled some distance to attend the wedding to our new, small home for a party the next day. We'd stocked up on lots of food and booze, but all they wanted were cups of tea and coffee. Apparently, they'd drunk a lot more alcohol at the wedding than we had!

We had a fabulous honeymoon throughout the South Island of New Zealand. I returned to my job and Kim to his

PhD. I was typing it for him, at his lab in the evenings. All 50,000 words! My complaining was overcome by all the hard work he was doing to produce the science. Little did we know that he was setting up our future on that publication.

We'd been married for about six months, and I remember vividly the day I got a call in the office from Kim.

"Are you sitting down?"

OMG, what was this? Was our marriage over? I thought we were doing well. "Yes, I am, now."

"Well, you know how you've been typing the name Dr. John B. West in a lot of the references in my thesis."

"Yes ..."

"And you know he's the head of Physiology at the University of California, San Diego, and recognized worldwide for his work?"

"Yes."

"Well, he's just offered me a job."

"In San Diego?"

"Yes, in La Jolla, where the university is based."

Holy crap. I was glad I was sitting down.

The position as a post-doctoral assistant physiologist depended on the completion of Kim's PhD thesis. Dr. West had led the 1981 American Medical Research Expedition to Mount Everest, when the first physiological measurements on the summit were made. He was exploring the next plateau—space. How do the lungs perform in zero gravity? The team in his lab needed a physiologist with an engineering bent. Kim fitted the description. What a thrill and an honor! But also, what an upheaval. Bernard's prophecy was coming true.

CHAPTER 17

But flies an eagle flight, bold and forth on, leaving no tract behind.
Timon of Athens

W e discussed Kim's job proposition for hours. In his wisdom, he suggested we go to San Diego for a year and see how we felt about life "over there." As I didn't have a work permit we knew things would be tougher for me. And so began the whirlwind of departure.

When Kim got the job offer, I'd already begun studying for a Teaching LTCL (Licentiate of Trinity College, London) in Speech and Drama. It was time to get a qualification that would give me greater freedom in my career choices. A talented teacher in Christchurch guided me through the requirements needed to develop a curriculum of classes for students and business folk, utilizing drama as the foundation. I also had to study four pieces—by Charles Dickens, the poet Percy Bysshe Shelley, Queen Margaret's famous speech from *Richard*

III, and Blanche DuBois's "moonlight swim" monologue in *A Streetcar Named Desire*. An examiner from Trinity flew out from London and I performed the pieces for him. It was both nerve-racking and exhilarating. I passed the examination. The theory exam to complete the diploma would have to wait.

After poignant family farewells, we departed Aotearoa in November 1983, three days after Kim had delivered his oral PhD examination. We packed copies of his thesis, a pair of sheets, two coffee mugs, some cutlery, a Christmas cake baked by my sister, and a wing and a prayer. We stopped off in Honolulu on the way to slow down, relax, and get used to the idea that we had left the shores of our native country. Looking back on photos of those three wonderful days, we look like shell-shocked Beverly Hillbillies!

We arrived in Los Angeles in the late afternoon. Kim's New Zealand colleague met us and drove us to San Diego. The dense stream of headlights facing us on the freeway and the red lights we followed provoked only one thought from me: "I will *never* drive in this country."

At the end of the first week in San Diego, we'd found a furnished apartment and bought a car. So much for the "not driving" decision. On the Monday of our second week, Kim was picked up very early in the morning by a colleague. They drove to San Fernando Valley to start developing the experiment instruments. They returned on Friday night. That went on for seven weeks. It was tough being alone in a new country. I knew no one, couldn't work as I didn't have a permit or a Social Security card, and our money was very tight. We had bought a tiny TV, so I did aerobics with an instructor on the screen, then walked around University Town Center just to be with people. A few may have commented on the "creepy woman who smiled at me today while I was out shopping!"

I cried a lot. I was homesick. I especially missed my mother, sister, and the children. America is an English-speaking country, but I didn't feel as though we spoke the same language. Feelings of self-doubt invaded. "Can I adapt?" "I've lived in England, can I do it here?" "What on earth will I do in San Diego?" "Will I let Kim down?" I was lonely too. I'd been used to being surrounded by a circle of friends. In this new world, I didn't have any.

To stop feeling sorry for myself in San Diego, I plunged into volunteering. I taught English to a Japanese student at UCSD. I signed up to volunteer at the Veterans Administration Hospital. My first task was explained to me by a senior nurse. "I need you to pass water."

Good grief! I'd signed up to help, not for urine testing. But we soon got that sorted out and I was off on my rounds, changing the water jugs in the wards. I met men who had fought for our freedom in WWII. What resilient men they were. They loved hearing my New Zealand accent.

"I fought alongside Kiwis in the trenches," said one gentleman. Half of his face was missing. I bought him cigarettes even though they were forbidden. He needed to indulge one bad habit after all he'd endured.

I attended a volunteer meeting at the San Diego Repertory Theatre. They were looking for a team to deliver a fundraiser to build a new space. To this day, I'm not sure how I got elected to chair the committee! But I met my best American friend, Carol, whom I adore to this day. I also volunteered at the Old Globe Theatre to be near artists. And it was through the Globe that I got my first job.

I had written several letters to the INS begging them for a work permit. No word came back. In desperation I wrote again and, in this letter, advised them that I needed a job (and the money) while my husband worked for NASA. I had a work permit in three weeks! NASA and the space shuttle programs were magic words in 1984.

On the day I got the permit, I baked a cake and bought a cheap bottle of champagne to treat my friends at the Globe. One of them asked me not to look for a job in the paper. Molly said, "I have a connection at the *San Diego Union* (the city's main newspaper), and I believe they're looking for a personal assistant for one of the editors." She was right. I was interviewed, Bernard was called to provide a reference, and I got the job!

What a place to work! In a buzzing, thriving newsroom, I got to know 120 people. A whole world of opportunities opened. One of the senior journalists was so renowned that notable people came to his office for interviews. He brought them all to meet *me*! Jackie Collins, Mitzi Gaynor, and Raymond Burr were three of them. What a thrill. I was mature enough now not to get tongue-tied.

For five years I worked in that newsroom. I made friends who I'm still in contact with today. I gained so much, not only in knowledge but in confidence. I had a series of columns published in the newspaper. I was invited to write and deliver commentaries on the topic of my choice on KPBS Radio in San Diego. That led to an audition for KPBS TV. They accepted me. I was ecstatic! I interviewed (live) the guests who came to the studio to help the nonprofit station raise necessary funding. Evenings spent with Patti LuPone or Sarah Brightman, twice with John Tesh, the chef Andrew Weil, musician Paul Anka, and more, were the thrill of a lifetime. And "the stars" were all gracious, kind, and a lot of fun!

I'd always harbored a desire to be on radio and television. Little did I know that I'd show up on both. I didn't know that I was capable of hosting on TV until I auditioned. It was a big risk for the station and for me, and outside my comfort zone. Some of my success was about being in the right place at the right time. Some of it came from my passion. Much of it came from taking risks and following dreams. Life ain't a dress rehearsal! This is the real and only thing.

CHAPTER 18

To be or not to be, that is the question.
Hamlet

It was time to complete the theory half of my LTCL. I was getting an itch that needed scratching. I was ready to change my career by myself, for myself, yet in the big picture, for others. I contacted Trinity College in London, and as luck would have it, there was a Fellow of the College in Costa Mesa, California, about 80 miles north of San Diego. The college sent me old exam papers and contacted the Fellow. I got advice from my teacher in Christchurch as to what to study, and I was off. Except that I *had* to study; not my forte, especially at the end of a full workday.

I would crawl up the stairs after dinner, spread the papers on the bed, and set to work. If I tried to leave before the requisite two hours set by Kim, he would stand at the bottom of the stairs with his arms across them, a stern face, and an admonishment, "You can't come down yet!" Little did he know that I would go back to the bedroom, lie down on the floor, and nap!

Kim drove me to Costa Mesa on the day of the exam. The Fellow invited me into his living room, where he had set up a table and chair beside a bookshelf that was loaded with the classics—many of the tomes I'd been studying! Then he went out for lunch! Boy, that was an honesty test. I could have found every answer I needed on that shelf! But I didn't peek. Imagine the guilt that would have produced!

I failed that exam by two marks, which was a real bummer. I had to wait for six months to sit it again. This time I passed! Great excitement and more calls for champagne. I finally had a qualification.

Not having a degree, diploma, or qualification didn't make me any less of a person. I know dozens of people worldwide who don't have college degrees, yet they do have responsible, fulfilling jobs and lives. However, the feeling I got when I completed my diploma was exhilarating.

So now, what to do with the LTCL? I would start a business where I could provide public speaking skills for individuals and groups. In 1988 I advised my newspaper boss that I would be leaving at the end of the year. There was a bit of commotion and sadness on both sides. However, I knew I'd made the right decision.

I received a "summons" from the editor in chief of the paper, Herb Klein, to meet him in his office. Now, I knew Herb quite well, as he frequently visited my editor, but this was out of the blue and unexpected. "What the hell have I *done*?" I thought. There goes the guilt again!

As it turned out, it was a meeting filled with fortune. Herb knew I was going to leave the newspaper to open a business. "I would like to introduce you to your first client!"

"Wow, thank you," I stammered, overwhelmed by his generosity.

Michael Copley, the stepson of the deceased Union-Tribune publisher, had been invited to speak at the opening of a library carrying his father's name and required some coaching in public speaking.

"Would you be willing to work with him?"

"I'd be delighted!"

My initial confidence was quickly followed by thoughts of doubt! "Was I up to this? Would Michael think me a sham? What if I failed?" There goes that impostor syndrome again!

Michael and I worked together for a few weeks. As I built his confidence, he built mine. He gave me a glowing testimonial—a great gift that helped to build my credibility. The Copley name is very well known in San Diego. Michael and I are friends to this day; I respect him highly.

CHAPTER 19

It is not in the stars to hold our destiny but in ourselves.
Julius Caesar

On my fortieth birthday, I drove to the business licensing office in downtown San Diego to register Prisk Communication. That felt powerful. I was a business owner! On the way home, I bought cakes and champagne. (My fallback choices!) That evening, when Kim returned from work, I rushed to tell him. We cracked open the bubbly and celebrated. Then with his perpetual practicality he said, "Owning a business means having clients; you don't have any." Damn! Why did he always say the right thing when I was up the wrong tree!

Two friends at the newspaper had expressed interest in learning public speaking skills. I approached them.

"Would you let me teach you the skills in my living room?"

"Only if you let us pay you," came the reply.

"All right then, how about $5.00 per class?"

"We should be paying more, but we accept."

It was stimulating planning the classes. I helped them craft speeches for specific audiences. I taught them breathing and relaxation techniques, and of course delivery skills. The teaching was exhilarating. I felt "on top of my game" and very fulfilled.

When the classes concluded, I gave them evaluation forms. Of course, I asked them to be very critical. The "I'm not good enough" syndrome again. They were fair and honest, and the response to my question "Should I operate a public speaking consultancy?" was followed by a resounding "Yes!" I will be forever grateful to these women.

Believing in myself has always been harder than having friends or family believe in me. One of life's most important lessons is to respect and care for the self. I am on this earth for a purpose, just as you are. Before we can fully realize that purpose, we must love ourselves.

This has been the hardest lesson for me, but one that I'm getting ahold of as I grow older. Nourishing, nurturing, and knowing myself takes time, courage, and empathy. As the lessons weren't provided to me early in life, I've taken longer than most to achieve a strong sense of self.

It was time to move forward! I enrolled in a series of workshops at the Small Business Administration. I learned how to develop a strategic plan, design a logo, understand financial planning (oh boy), and how to seek and engage clients. As part of the program, I was allocated a business mentor, a man whose lessons I remember to this day.

"Remember to pay yourself, no matter how small the amount. And dress for business, even though you're at home. It will show up in your demeanor. Imagine that you're sitting on the twentieth floor of a building. Everyone on every floor is working for Prisk Communication." Sterling advice. We met weekly, and I learned so much from him. He was practical, forceful, and kind. Just what I needed.

Mentoring is an underrated art. To have someone walking beside me, sharing their lessons and losses, and applying creative skill and imagination to my needs was paramount to my success. We call them coaches in sports and other activities, and the designation provides the same result for those to whom it's applied: a greater understanding of the whole game, the parts required to make it work, the ability to deal with negatives, the importance of teamwork, the look of success and how to repeat it.

Women in business, I believe, absolutely must have a mentor or mentors. A person who provides positive feedback not only for the business, but for the owner. Many women doubt themselves and their potential; I know, I've met them over the years. They have said things to me like: "I would love to start a business, but I don't have the confidence." "I'm not sure who would want my services." "You seem so successful; I could never be that." The latter comment receives a firm response from me: "If I can do it, you can do it. I am no different."

My business continued to develop and grow. And I thought I was too. But nagging doubts and fears about not being good enough, not being smart enough, not being competent enough often overtook my thoughts, despite all the self-talk and advice I gave others.

Kim and I were doing plenty of socializing and making new friends, and every time one of them talked fondly about their father, I grew madly envious, and sad. I never mentioned mine. In conversations by phone with my mother, I sensed that things at home were not good. My father used to get on the line and make gushing statements about me, the world, and how he and my mother were, but I knew they were lies. My mother would tell me in her letters of his untruths, escapades, and incidents. They gnawed at my heart and stomach. And that stomach of mine was becoming a pain!

FIFTH DECADE

1989–1999

BREAKING

REFLECTIONS

The Roaring Forties! They come upon you like the winds in the southern hemisphere that blow at gale force. There are three variables involved: warm air movements, the Earth's rotation, and the near absence of relevant landmasses.

A lot of air has passed through your lungs by this stage of your life. The Earth has rotated around the Sun forty-plus times. There'll be days when you feel as though you've lost sight of your anchoring cove. Your safe place. If you plan to live till you're eighty, you're halfway there! Scary stuff? Nah? Only if you let it be.

You've witnessed history being written. You've told people to "f— off" if you don't like their attitude. Your dress style is yours. Your business colleagues respect and appreciate you. You appreciate yourself.

If the kids have left the nest and you're still happy with your partner, your sex life is probably better than ever. You hold opinions on every topic and aren't afraid to state them.

You've become altruistic and have found causes that you want to support. You don't feel too guilty about taking time out for yourself at the spa or a fine-dining restaurant. You appreciate your friends; they seem very together. And if they're not, you're full of great advice for them.

Carl Jung said, "Life really begins at forty. Up until then, you are just doing research." Never stop the research. Never stop the learning. But do pause and remember that this can also be a challenging time of your life. Take care of your parts, as they can break. Not just your heart, but your brain too.

CHAPTER 20

The web of our life is of a mingled yarn, good and ill together.
All's Well That Ends Well

Networking isn't everyone's favorite sport. For introverts, it can be excruciating. It requires a lot of effort, patience, and listening—often to conversations that bore you to death. I'm lucky that I love it! The idea of walking into a room full of strangers to talk about business is exhilarating. So, I networked like crazy. And joined organizations that would boost my business. NAWBO (The National Association of Women Business Owners) was one of them. It allowed me to meet with successful leaders who nurtured my hopes that I could join their ranks. They guided, coached, and mentored me. They gave me the confidence to step outside my comfort zone. One of them furnished me with an office, at no charge. They offered connections to other organizations.

The former US Secretary of State for President Bill Clinton, Madeleine Albright, once said: "There's a special place in hell for women who don't support other women." My networking connections are all going to heaven!

I began speaking at conferences, business events, and organizational gatherings in San Diego. Mostly pro bono. I had two things firmly on my side: the support of other women and KPBS. My on-screen interviews helped me with *my* interviews. I received welcoming comments like: "I know you, I've seen you on TV." That built trust, one of the most successful components of a business.

I vividly remember one speaking event. There were about a hundred people present, but no stage, riser, or microphone.

"I'm going to have to be creative here," I thought, as I kicked off my shoes, stepped onto a chair, put my fingers in my mouth, and whistled. I projected my voice and got everyone's attention. The audience loved it; they laughed, participated in the exercises, and we all had a great evening.

Albright again: "It took me quite a long time to develop a voice, and now that I have it, I am not going to be silent." Such an important lesson for all women! Use. Your. Voice.

This rhythm continued for the first year of my business. I grossed $1,500 in year-end revenues! I was ecstatic. (I almost doubled that to $2,800 in the second year. I was on a roll!) These amounts are small, but their resulting confidence priceless. I was my own boss, creating my own work schedules, conducting my own business, and reaping the small but meaningful assets!

It was time to branch out in a new direction—the University of California, San Diego Extension Studies Department. I met with the Arts and Humanities director to discuss my proposal of an evening class in public speaking. She invited me to develop a course for engineers, and for the next three years I facilitated *Communicating Your Best*, a six-week class of three hours one evening per week. Many engineers participated in those classes, and it was through their goodwill that the doors to corporate America began to open.

One evening, one of the participants told me about a brand-new construction company, headquartered in Redwood City, California, that was about to open an office in San Diego. He'd been doing some work with the company.

"They're looking for a presentations coach to help them with business development. Would you like me to throw your hat in the ring?"

"Throw my hat, coat, *and* gloves in the ring!" This was exciting!

My interview was conducted by the founders of DPR Construction, Doug, Peter, and Ron (DPR), and about fifteen others who constituted the San Diego team.

"Can you design a workshop for participants that focuses on communicating with customers, delivering effective presentations to win construction projects, plus all the elements that go with these goals?"

"Yes, I can!"

Although my confidence was shaky and some of the old messages of doubt began to creep in, I shooed them away and began the design in earnest. I learned the importance of believing in my unique talents, my abilities, and my personal power.

DPR provided me with six local leaders to "test run" my classes—six very smart guys who certainly tested me, in the kindest possible way. We had a great deal of fun, despite their horror at being videotaped. They judged the classes a success, so we scheduled more for San Diego. A representative from the

Redwood City office joined us to observe. I was invited to fly north to deliver classes there. DPR continued to open offices across the US. I was asked to travel to them all and provide the same education. Prisk Communication was off and flying!

Today, DPR Construction has thirty offices across the US and internationally; their annual revenues top $7 billion. DPR Construction will forever be in my heart for the years I have collaborated with the fabulous people in the company. Also, for how much they believed in me and my training.

I met my mentee-to-be, Samuel, at DPR. After he'd attended one of my workshops, we talked for ages.

"One day I'd love to do what you do," he said.

"May I mentor you?" I asked. He replied enthusiastically in the affirmative.

We discussed his dreams for his future. How he could become a coach and trainer. We planned a workshop together. Audiences enjoyed the combination of a Gen X and a baby boomer at the front of the room. Two diverse viewpoints!

After about six months of my mentoring, he slammed down the lid of his laptop and said, "I'm sick of talking about me! I want to talk about Jenni!"

That was a surprise. But a great one. He invited me to set goals for myself for the next twelve months. I set five. (Get back on stage, learn to play golf, get better at computer technology, get better at promoting my business, and like myself more.) He guided me through them, and I "passed."

He wanted to see the world. I eventually booted him out of the country for a long, invigorating trip. He came back a changed man. Today he's married with two daughters. Lucky girls!

DPR asked if I would sign an exclusive contract, meaning that if other construction companies contacted me while I was working with DPR, I would turn them down. I agreed, and we continued this arrangement for two-plus years. They were some of the best years of my life. I had never dreamed that I would spend so much time in the building industry. When the exclusivity ended, I was contacted by many other construction companies to provide training for them.

While I was flying around the country, meeting tons of new people and passionately sharing all I knew about presenting, my body started yelling for help. My periods had become very heavy, my gut was cramping, and (much to my delight) I was losing weight. But not in the right way. I had the onset of IBS (irritable bowel syndrome), which I tried to ignore, but Mother Nature had other ideas that she would soon activate.

CHAPTER 21

If by chance I talk a little wild, forgive me; I had it from my father.
Henry VIII

On June 5, 1991, the space shuttle *Columbia* carrying Kim's laboratory experiment launched from the Kennedy Space Center. One for the history books! It was the fifth dedicated Spacelab mission (Spacelab Life Sciences-1) and the first mission committed solely to life sciences, using the habitable module. Six body systems were investigated, and Kim's involvement was with the cardiovascular/cardiopulmonary (heart, lungs, and blood vessels) experiment. And there were two female astronauts on board! That made my heart soar.

Kim had to be in Houston to connect with the crew when they were utilizing the lung function system. Out of the blue, he surprised me.

"I've bought you an airline ticket to the Cape (Canaveral) so you can watch the launch, live!"

I almost went into orbit myself at this fantastic news!

The launch suffered a few technical delays, so I had to tough it out in a beach house beside the Atlantic. The weather was very warm, so I swam in the ocean and soaked up the sun until the day of launch.

I will never forget the experience of watching (and feeling) the shuttle leave its earthly pad and glide flawlessly into the ether. We were seated in the viewing stands three miles away. When 90,000 tons of fuel ignited, the enormous thrust at liftoff surged through my body from bottom to top. My feet started vibrating, then the rest of my body shook, and my heart began pounding heavily. They were a surreal few moments. The shuttle soared skyward and slipped through the sultry clouds on its journey to space. Despite my shaking hands, I managed to capture five good photos, which I had framed, with a plaque, for Kim on his return home.

Unfortunately, not all was fun and games for me. Women carry a womb, and all the necessary bits and pieces and hormones, for most of our lives. Without them, our functions wouldn't be balanced. Nor would our brains. Sadly, during my professionally productive years, my health was in decline. Some days I couldn't leave the house because my periods were so severe. I got scared and thought I might bleed to death. It turned out I was carrying forty-plus fibroids in my uterus, and any woman who has suffered with them knows they are not ideal companions. At some stage in our lives, we have all felt debilitated. Perhaps through loss of a job or a loved one, insufficient money, bullying, losing out on that top job, or bad health that hampers our forward progress. The latter was my burden to shoulder.

My doctor sent me to a surgeon who very swiftly removed those suckers, much to my physical and mental relief. However, the surgeon advised, "There's a very large fibroid growing behind your uterus that one day soon will require you to have a hysterectomy."

This was devastating news, as Kim and I had been trying to conceive. And time was running out on my age.

Surgeons can replace a knee or a hip, repair torn ligaments, even mend a heart, but when a womb is damaged, it must go; there's no replacement. Yet. Hopefully there will be one day.

I couldn't fully focus on my professional clients because I was afraid that something internal would combust and have me rushing from the room leaving blood all over my chair. Some days I felt dizzy and lost my concentration. Couple that with the IBS, and I was in a right old state!

Fibroids are sometimes referred to by other names—leiomyomas (lie-o-my-O-muhs) or myomas—which sound almost romantic. I can assure you they are not. This invading enemy made me very tired too. I've always been full of energy, so this was an annoyance. Over the years, I've had many women friends talk to me about their fibroids and how nervous they are about having them removed. Do not be! Deal with them or they will deal with you. And if you're trying to conceive, it's even more imperative that you get them out.

While I was trying to cope with the invasion, another major event took place. My father died. He had been confined to the house for a couple of years following the amputation of his left leg below the knee. He was diabetic and took terrible care of himself—irregular and inappropriate meals, copious candies and cakes, and erratic sleep patterns. It always surprised me, as he'd been such a fitness fanatic in his younger days.

One evening in June 1993, my sister called me in San Diego with the news of my father's death. I went numb. All those years of being afraid of him tumbled through my head. I didn't feel loss, but I did feel some sadness. He *had* given life to me. I was soon on a plane to New Zealand.

CHAPTER 22

Cowards die many times before their deaths ...
Julius Caesar

My thoughts on the sixteen-hour flight back to New Zealand were all over the place. I was wound up tighter than a tick. Would life be different now that he was dead? Would there be a different kind of atmosphere in my mother's house now that he was gone? Would I start to heal, or would he continue to haunt me? And what about his molestation of a young boy who lived next door to us in our original family home that had recently surfaced? The boy's father had written letters to Dad, and before he died had stood in the street outside my parents' home yelling, "I will get you for what you have done to my son. I will take you to court." Would I have to face this enraged father and deal with the outbursts? My stomach was tied up in knots all the way to New Zealand, and I barely slept.

And how would my mother be? Would she have taken to her bed and popped a valium or two? Would she have faced the truth about her husband after being in denial for so many years?

As soon as I landed, I asked to be taken to the funeral home to see my father's body. I had to know that he was quieted now, no longer a risk. I fainted at the first sight of his normally resilient presence, which had become a contracted corpse.

Seeing him in his casket was an odd sensation. You know that feeling when you pull a band-aid off and stare at the wound, curious about the result? It felt a bit like that for me. I don't know that I fully realized that he was gone forever. However, I gained liberation from my father's sins by way of remonstrations directly to his silent, dead body, and thus my healing process began.

At his funeral, my sister spoke eloquently. She included some remarks about Dad not being the charming man everyone thought he was, that he had a very dark side too. This was courageous and raised a few eyebrows. Most of those present thought he could charm the birds out of the trees.

Death affects us all differently. Depending on the relationship we have shared with the deceased, grief comes in assorted packages. For some, the grieving period is short and sad; for others it is everlasting. But whatever the situation, grief must be dealt with in the most appropriate way for the people affected. Grief out is better for our health than grief that stays locked inside. However, there's no panacea. I don't remember if I cried much when my father died. For my grandmother and mother, I wept buckets.

Flying back to San Diego, I had many hours to analyze my anguish. What did I really feel? Were my feelings those of relief or sadness? Why was I experiencing a weird "high"? Did I feel any guilt at leaving my mother again? No, I didn't! Because the bane of her life had been removed and she was now free. I hoped that I too would be free, but sadly that wasn't the case.

CHAPTER 23

The miserable have no other medicine. But only hope.
Measure for Measure

Three days after my return to San Diego and my reunion with Kim, I woke gasping in the middle of the night, trying to climb up the bedroom wall.

"He's coming to get me. I've got to get away." The "he," of course, was my father. And so, the downward spiral began.

The IBS was increasing, the weight loss persisted, I didn't sleep well and cried a lot. I developed agoraphobia, which ended the lovely long walks we used to take in the canyon near our home. Kim was very supportive and caring and made sure I saw my doctor regularly, but he was traveling a lot as the space program was at its zenith.

I was tested for fertility and came through with flying colors. Kim was tested and came through with an alarmingly low sperm count. His doctor wondered if he'd been exposed to radiation at some time in his life. We haven't been able to solve that one. The doctor suggested artificial insemination, but HIV/AIDS was rife and the testing wasn't 100 percent safe, so I refused.

Meanwhile, the enemy in my uterus was growing exponentially, and it was time to face the music. I had to have the hysterectomy. Because I was forty-two, the surgeon advised it would be wise to remove my ovaries too. Ovarian cancer, should it develop, can be difficult to diagnose without a womb. And as he said somewhat unkindly, "Your years of childbearing are over!" I was crushed, deflated, and depressed. But it was my fate.

The surgery was successful. I entered the hospital premenopausal and departed in menopause. Kim was a marvelous nurse and looked after me constantly for the first couple of weeks. I healed well physically but not so well mentally. While I was taking a very mild dose of estrogen to counteract my lack of ovaries, it wasn't helping my mental condition. My thoughts were dark and desperate. I started to lose interest in things I loved. I could no longer play the clown and cover it up. I returned to my business but didn't manage it very well. I couldn't keep focus. I felt inadequate. I didn't really enjoy the coaching and teaching anymore. And all the while, when I spoke with the surgeon about the difficulties, he wasn't the slightest bit interested. He just wanted to know how the wound was healing!

Ovary removal (oophorectomy) is not to be taken lightly. Ovaries control so many of a woman's body functions, including and especially the emotional range. We discussed the pros and cons with the doctor and read all the resources available when making the decision. But we didn't learn enough about the types of medications available following the surgery. The brain also needs to get through the change successfully. The dose of estrogen I was given was too low for me and my mental state.

Still, there were bright spots. Out of the blue, a theatre director called and asked if I would voice-coach an Australian play, *The Sum of Us*. Actor Russell Crowe made his debut appearance in the film of the same name. I reminded the director that I was a New Zealander, not an Ozzie, and she replied, "Well, you all sound the same to Americans!" So, I joined the cast for rehearsals. What a great group of people! We had a blast and I got them as close to the accent as I could.

During rehearsals, the young man playing the lead role and I connected very deeply. He was one of the most beautiful men I have ever laid eyes on. If you can imagine a mix of James Dean and Elvis Presley, then you've got JD. During Kim's travels and my roller coaster ride of emotions, JD and I visited too many bars, drank from too many bottles, and shared too many late nights. He was gay, and loved taking me to dive bars where we would dance, wildly, like there was no tomorrow. And for him there wasn't. He got HIV-AIDS. In 2006 he died, and my heart broke. While he was dying, he helped me to live—albeit not in the healthiest or wisest way.

I learned from JD about the struggles and suffering that came with being gay; about not being accepted; about being bullied and cast out; about being rejected by family. One night I remember him saying, "If I could start my life all over again, I certainly wouldn't choose this one." He helped me to understand the challenges facing my gay friends.

At the closing-night performance of *The Sum of Us*, we had a rip-roaring party. Kim was away, so I took a couple of bottles of champagne as my date. During the evening, I sang a drunken version of "Big Spender" using one of the bottles as a microphone. A voice called out across the room, "You, Jenni, will be Madame Arcati in *Blithe Spirit!*" It was the director. I called her the next day to see if she meant it. She did. So, I went into rehearsals for the best role of my theatrical life.

We opened at the North Coast Repertory Theatre in San Diego for a four-week run that was loved by critics and audiences alike. I was as nervous as hell every night before my first entrance, in emerald green satin harem pants, a long loose top, and matching turban. I also wore huge gold earrings. I didn't have pierced ears (still don't), so they were tenuously hanging on. During a scene, when the owner of the stately home Arcati was visiting to perform a séance handed me a cocktail, one of the earrings fell down the front of my top. Now, audiences see everything, and that was obviously not part of the script, so I had to ad-lib like mad as I fished it out and put it back on again.

During another scene, I delivered my lines, then sat smugly on the edge of a sofa in a silence that seemed to go on forever. All the while, the lead male actor was offering all sorts of prompts, and I kept thinking how good it was that I was safe; it wasn't my line that was missing. He walked over to me, clapped me hard on the shoulder and bellowed, "Madame Arcati, is there anywhere you would like us to move to in this room?" Holy shit, it *was* my line!! Kim was in the audience that night; he knew the line, and it was all he could do to stop himself from calling it out.

Yet again theatre had saved my sanity, but it wasn't enough for what lay ahead.

CHAPTER 24

Discomfort guides my tongue and bids me speak of nothing but despair.
Richard II

Kim continued to travel, and I fell into a deep depression. I turned even more toward alcohol. Copious amounts made me feel better. Everything was starting to lose color. Sleep was a fading friend. It was frightening, and I felt very alone.

I fell apart in the children's clothing department of a major store. I'd been pulling out various tiny outfits to purchase for a baby shower. The more I looked at the clothing, the sadder I became. I had hoped so much that one day I'd shop for clothes for *our* baby. The tears started falling thick and fast. I put my head down on the clothing rack and sobbed. A kindhearted woman who was shopping nearby came over and put her arm around my shoulders.

"Can I help you?" she asked. Through my blubbering I told her my story. She was sympathetic. "You don't have to buy these clothes, you know. In fact, you don't even have to go to that baby shower." She was right. I left the shop empty-handed, phoned in my apologies, and didn't venture out to a shower until my mental health returned.

If we couldn't have a child naturally, why didn't we adopt? We did investigate every available avenue: church agencies, Romania (where children were dying in orphanages while chained to their cots), and private agencies. We even hired a lawyer in New Zealand to see if we could adopt a Kiwi baby. The wait in that situation would have been two years; Kim would have had to give up his career in the US so we could live in New Zealand again and be put in the pool for a child, with no guarantee of a baby at the end of the wait. It was nerve-racking and heartbreaking.

After all we went through, I refrain from asking friends or family when or if they're going to have kids. I don't know what they're up against and how much pain they might be in. And I will never ask, "Why don't you adopt?" It's none of my business! (Similar to rubbing a pregnant woman's belly when you don't know her.)

We were frequently asked when we would start a family. On one occasion, Kim blurted out a great reply: "We tried it once and it made me sick ..." He repeated it whenever necessary. No one ever asked us anything beyond that! Now, when friends comment about the fact that we're off on another trip somewhere in the world, our joint response is, "Yep, we're spending our kids' inheritance." That shuts them up!

I may jest, but it wasn't funny. The idea of two humans creating another is the most fundamental anthropological yearning. There's an assumption that when two people of any sexual orientation marry or form a partnership, they will add to that union. And it can be a living hell when it doesn't happen. Be gentle on yourself and others around this question. Support anyone's decision to *not* have children, and especially support those who have tried.

Life has a way of channeling a life toward a new life. New callings appear when the pain has healed. Nowadays I fawn over every baby I see. I adore them all. And especially the beautiful baby girl a friend "gave" to us as our goddaughter, the week of my hysterectomy.

But all the empathy, all the gifts of kindness, and all my struggling to reach the light from the bottom of a very dark well didn't assuage the desperate feelings of hopelessness, inadequacy, and despair I felt.

CHAPTER 25

Death rock me asleep.
King Henry IV

One balmy evening when Kim was away on yet another trip, I climbed the stairs to our bedroom. I carried four bottles of wine and a large bottle of aspirin. Time to end it all. If I couldn't be a mum, then what was my purpose? I probably wasn't much of a wife either. And my clients could surely live without me.

I sat on our bathroom floor, lit a few candles, and started drinking. After finishing the first bottle, I took some of the pills, then drank more wine. My tears fell like rain. Until I heard a voice—a very strong voice and one I recognized. It was my grandmother's. I sat up and looked around. Of course, she wasn't there.

"Jen!" I heard. "Jen, you're needed!"

It was over. I was still there. Her words resonated in my stupefied brain.

"You're needed."

I didn't really take in what they meant, but I'd heard them. I curled up on the floor, sobbed my heart out, and the next thing I knew, it was morning. And I *was* still there.

I came to very groggy, confused, hungover, shivering, and ashamed, but alive. Now what? All the plans I thought I'd ended would have to start up again. How on earth would I do that? Would my experience be written all over me? Would I be considered weird if people found out? Would clients cast me aside because of what I tried to do? Would my friends like me less? Who was that woman staring back at me from the mirror? What did she stand for now? Was everything she had done a lie? And how would I explain it to Kim? I filled a hot water bottle, crawled between the sheets, and slept for hours. I hoped that tomorrow would bring answers.

Suicide is a very serious matter. When a person reaches this state, despondency and desperation are overwhelming. It can be very challenging to talk to the afflicted person. You may not have seen the symptoms because they've cleverly hidden them. I am one of these survivors. No one in my circle imagined I would try to take my life. I hid my tears and anguish. I kept believing I would be OK. My dear friend, Carol, knew I was low, but she didn't know I was at rock bottom. Even Kim, with all our closeness, had not suspected. He had become used to my "manic" personality, where I would be on a "high" for periods of time or have a decreased need for sleep, talk faster than usual, or feel extremely restless or impulsive. This was all put down to my "high energy" and not seen as trouble brewing.

An episode of attempted suicide isn't easy to get over. Just because I came back from the brink didn't mean that I was cured or healed. Just because I was alive didn't mean I was living. My nerves were raw, my sensitivity to negative remarks and encounters was heightened, and my self-confidence was very low.

By now, I had an attractive office in a professional building complex where I coached my individual clients. I was proud of that office and the surroundings, but not of what was going on in my body. The IBS was really bad by now. It was exacerbated when I was alone with a male client. I had to leave the door open during the session to provide a means of "escape." Several times during a session, I would make some lame excuse that I needed to retrieve a fax or a document, and instead would rush to the bathroom. In one hour, this could happen up to five times. To my surprise, my clients continued to seek my services!

One day, when I was coaching a client (a gentleman I'd known for several years), I opened my mouth to speak and the only thing that came forth was tears. Copious tears. A veritable floodgate opened, drowning the papers on my desk. *OMG*, I thought, *what the hell is going on?* I tried to apologize but couldn't speak. Fortunately, he was sympathetic and asked if he could help. I mumbled no, and he suggested that I call my doctor. Then he left my office, but not before offering to drive me wherever I needed to go. Of course, even through all this, "miss independence" said, "No, thanks, I'll be fine!!" I was a good liar.

When people offer to help, they usually mean it. I should have accepted his offer. One of my favorite quotes is from Ray Kroc of San Diego, who made McDonald's the giant it is today: "None of us is as good as all of us." And that includes not only friends and family, but services too. I was about to find out how the power of good medical help, friends, and services would change my life!

CHAPTER 26

Sufferance is the badge of all our tribe.
The Merchant of Venice

I did call my doctor on that pivotal day. He was very concerned and asked if I could drive. Of course I could! He
referred me to a counselor. I remember walking into her office
and for the next 45 minutes spewing out all my troubles. I
talked and talked and talked. I poured out everything that had
happened over the years: my father and the hideous things he
had done to me and to other youngsters, moving to another
country, my surgeries, infertility, and my shame about my
attempt at suicide. I blubbered, I trembled, and I talked.

At the end of those minutes, I stood up and said, "I've taken
up too much of your time. You must have many people with
greater needs than mine. I'll go now."

"Sit down!" came the firm response. "You're not going anywhere until I've referred you to a clinical psychiatrist!"

This filled me with more shame. A psychiatrist! Only really sick and troubled people need them. And then I realized: I was sick and troubled. And I sure as hell needed help.

So, I sat. And I waited. Eventually the counselor reached the professional she was calling. "You can go straight to this address. Dr. Lewis will see you right away. She has a gap between appointments."

My session with the "shrink" was excellent. She quickly diagnosed my needs and prescribed an antidepressant medication. I was now a full-blown depressed person! What would life be like from now on? Would I be changed? Could I go back to normal? Well, let me tell you, this was the best prescription I've ever had to fill. Within a few days, the barbed wire in my head started to unravel. My sense of taste and smell and the colors of the world returned to normal. I slept better. I ate better too, as food tasted yummy again. But best of all was the slow disappearance of fearful, inhibiting, and anxious thoughts. I could see straight and think straight. My life was starting to feel like every other normal person's life—clear and happy! I was no longer living at the bottom of that well, but slowly climbing up the slippery walls toward the light.

I take the medication to this day (with a few adjustments along the way), and it's been a literal lifesaver. I also know there's no stigma to swallowing that pill every night. Kim's life is better. Mine is infinitely better. And I can function on every level! Never be ashamed if you find yourself, a loved one, or a friend in this situation. It is an illness, not an embarrassment. It's treatable and must be treated. Good mental health means good physical and spiritual health, and the world looks a whole lot better. And you can continue to pursue the purpose that brought you here!

CHAPTER 27

Fortune brings in some boats that are not steer'd.
Cymbeline

Life began to show its riches again through an exciting opportunity to meet a hero. We frequently refer to all sorts of people as heroes because of deeds they have done. This is all good and fine if it doesn't become hackneyed. Merriam-Webster defines a hero as "a person who is admired for great or brave acts." As a child growing up in New Zealand, that's how I thought of Sir Edmund Hillary, the first conqueror of Mt. Everest in 1953.

Dr. John B. West, the instigator of our life in San Diego, was a close friend of Hillary. He was the physiologist on Sir Edmund Hillary's Silver Hut expedition in 1960–1961, and led the 1981 American Medical Research Expedition to Everest.

Ed was dining at the Wests' home, and we were invited to join them! Wow, what a thrill. When we met, I noticed his weathered face, solid jaw, and enormous hands. He regaled us with stories of his nonprofit work in the Himalayas and current activities. It wasn't appropriate to ask him about his experience of climbing Everest all those years ago. Anyway, I'm sure his reply would have been his famous one: "We knocked the bastard off!"

Unexpectedly, the role of the woman in *The Sum of Us* that I had dialect-coached a few years prior was offered to me. The production would run at a very small theatre in downtown San Diego that seated forty people. I was ecstatic. I loved the play, as it was such a rich story of the desperate need gay people have for acceptance. I too needed to be reaccepted.

The male lead, Morris, and I began our first scene together, arriving at his character's home after a first date. The director decided that Morris should carry me up the small aisle on his back. Now, I'm a woman of strong proportions, and that sounded impossible to me. But in the theatre world, there are answers for everything.

Before my character discovered the porn magazines in the bureau drawer, we had to share a passionate kiss. I'd been writing theatre reviews for Morris's online publication for a long time, and at every rehearsal he kept saying, "I can't kiss Jenni Prisk!"

"Oh yes you can," I said one night, and planted a doozy on him. He was in, boots and all, after that!

That production set me up for a role in *The Killing of Sister George,* staged at Diversionary Theatre, the long-established LGBTQ playhouse in San Diego. This time I played a gay woman, where the kissing scene was easy. I will say that women frequently have more overt courage than men when it comes to taking risks and crossing lines!

A role I will never forget was that of Alan Turing's mother in *Breaking the Code*. Also staged at Diversionary, this intense piece portrayed the life of the brilliant mathematician who cracked the German Enigma code at Bletchley Park during WWII. Turing was gay and was most likely more tortured by that than the decoding race. In one scene, he "came out" to his mother, which was breathlessly poignant to stage in a theatre where many in the audience had experienced the same scene themselves. Turing took his life; however, I'm grateful that he received a royal pardon in 2013 for saving the lives of thousands through his war work. And now his face is on the British £50 note!

Another personal sadness entered my life. My mother died. She'd been living in a rest home for some three years—three years of peace for her. I'd visited her in her new abode, where she was extremely happy: looked after from morning till night, with the company of others, meals cooked for her, and no husband to threaten her. But her heart expired, and with my sister at her side, she peacefully slipped the surly bonds of earth.

I returned to New Zealand for her funeral. Kim said to me on my return to San Diego, "Now we're both orphans." His parents had died much earlier than mine. The death of parents moves our place in the universe to a different sphere. We become the elders of our tribes. In our case, with no children to follow us, we are the last of our generation.

SIXTH DECADE

1999–2009

RISING

REFLECTIONS

You're in your fifties now, the golden years! That doesn't mean you sink with the sun every evening. In fact, far from it. You may have more energy now than you've ever had before. And more wrinkles than you had in your forties—but that's OK, they are lifelines. They express your life thus far, in all its fret and fun.

The lines between your eyebrows (that look as though someone skied down your forehead) have been formed from thinking hard, visioning, and listening carefully. Those around your eyes and mouth are from laughing and smiling. And from pain you've experienced too. Embrace them; they happen to everyone. Remember, you are born with the face that nature gave you, and you will die with the face you gave yourself (with perhaps a little help from Botox).

Keep up those exercises, as your body's starting to lose some of its flexibility and strength. And maintain your friendships, because they too are golden. Travel as much as you can while your legs will carry you to far-off places and your brain can fully absorb the experience.

And experiment on yourself and your style. How would new makeup look? Or a new "do?" Or different clothes? (But promise yourself you won't do the mutton-dressed-up-as-lamb approach!) Walk into a room and own it. Make your voice heard. Speak up against atrocities.

Fifty is half a hundred, and that's an impressive number in human terms. Give yourself a "high five" every morning and add some gratitude that you made it through the night. And if all else fails, tell people you're approaching fifty but you won't say from which direction!

CHAPTER 28

What light through yonder window breaks?
Romeo and Juliet

New opportunities began to show up. Frequently when there's been a climb up from the bottom of a well, a need arises to help others in their climb. Not long after my return to better health, I was approached by a friend who worked with people with disabilities. "Would you be willing to develop a public speaking course for these folks?"

At first, I was daunted. What did I know about teaching a course for young people who were differently abled? How would I handle it? It didn't take long for me to get over myself and start asking smarter questions, like "How would they like to learn? How can I bring out the best in each of them? What will I learn?"

Six eager students enrolled for the five-week course, held on Saturday mornings. They were brought to the teaching facility by caregivers or family. They were excited about the possibility of learning a new skill. I thought they'd be nervous about "exposing" themselves verbally in front of a small audience; however, the opposite was true. It was as though a dam burst for each of them and they released words and emotions they may not have shared before.

One young man with Down syndrome wrote and delivered a love poem, in iambic pentameter, to his caregiver. That broke all our hearts. A young woman talked about her dreams and desires for her life, which were just like yours and mine. She wanted to belong and feel needed. Her mother came to me on "graduation" day (they got certificates and chocolates) with tears welling in her eyes.

"You've no idea how this has changed my daughter. She could barely talk to anyone, let alone strangers, and now she's been in front of an audience and spoken eloquently."

That lovely woman had no idea how *I* had been changed!

The years were moving on, and we decided to celebrate the millennium in Napier, New Zealand. It's where the sun would first breach the horizon in that momentous new year. Several San Diegan friends asked us to contact them immediately when Solis appeared so they'd know we had survived Y2K, and so had the internet and the stock exchange!

The evening began with a spirited party at a cousin's home that went on till 3:00 a.m. Kim and I were sleeping on the landing and had barely hit the pillow when, just before dawn, the piercing sound of bagpipes blasted cruelly up the stairwell. Kim turned to me blearily and mumbled, "I'd like to put that chanter where the sun doesn't shine!"

We donned clothes, grabbed a glass of champagne (as you do in the middle of the night), and followed the piper to the neighbors to watch January 1, 2000, slip majestically and beautifully onto the horizon.

I was still coming to grips with not being a parent. Still battling some insecurities. But mostly enjoying good health, good friends, and plentiful work. Kim surprised me for my fiftieth birthday. He'd been traveling so much that he'd accumulated hundreds of frequent-flier miles, so he used them to book flights from New York to Paris and back on Concorde! What a spectacular experience! We were two of 100 passengers on the streamlined jet that flew at Mach 2.04 (twice the speed of sound) at 65,000 feet—so high that the atmosphere was purple, and we could see the curvature of the earth.

The plane was very hot because of the atmospheric friction outside the windows, and not very wide, so that being of larger proportions, Kim and I had to turn sideways to get down the aisle. The petite flight attendants wheeled a tiny cart filled with delicious French food and lots of champagne up and down that aisle during the more than three-hour flight.

Many of the passengers had experienced this trip many times before. That was obvious in the way they nonchalantly read their books or newspapers. Not so for us. We were like a couple of kids, sitting in every spare seat and looking out the windows, visiting the cockpit (in those days, it was accessible), standing under the Mach 2 digital sign for photos, and grinning our heads off at an experience that was literally out of this world! Concorde was grounded in 2003 after an accident on a runway. Interestingly, we received several "sympathy" messages from friends who felt connected to this magnificent machine through our trip.

We meandered our way through France, then joined a barge trip for five days in the Loire Valley. The surrounding countryside was bucolic. Rolling hills, golden flowers, and green riverbanks. The barge itself was trimmed with flower boxes and looked charming. We embarked into what I hoped would be peace and tranquility. However, as we received our welcoming glass of champagne, a loud voice proclaimed: "I know you! You're on KPBS TV!" A small group of people from San Diego were on the cruise, and lovely though they were, it meant that we spent much of the time in their company.

We returned home feeling refreshed and invigorated. I felt stronger and more positive. Turning fifty begins an important decade. It's the stage (hopefully) where a career or role is established, financial security exists, relationships are formed, children are mature and usually out of the nest, and new and different challenges can become appealing. Thoughts turn toward philanthropy and charitable organizations, or service to the community. My opportunity came up faster than I'd expected because of a creeping menace that was penetrating the planet in the form of extremism that was about to make one of its ugliest statements to the world.

CHAPTER 29

The night is long that never finds the day.
Macbeth

Most of the world remembers 9/11. None more than those of us living in the United States. On that inauspicious Tuesday, I was in Seattle, Washington, providing training for a client. I'd gone downstairs in my hotel for breakfast. As I don't turn on the TV when I wake up, I was completely unaware of the tragedy. In the elevator on my way back to my room, a woman was hyperventilating.

"Oh my God, have you seen the destruction in New York City? Planes have crashed into the Twin Towers! And all those people being killed, it's beyond imagination!"

I thought she was overreacting to some Hollywood movie until I turned on the TV. I too was overwhelmed by the horrific pictures that repeated endlessly throughout the day and into the night. The scenes were unbelievable. Who had the guts to fly planes into a building? Who conceived this unimaginable act of hatred? How many people who lived and worked in the Twin Towers would die?

I stayed in my room, glued to the TV. I started yelling. And crying. "Why is this happening on American soil? Who masterminded this attack? Would another city in the US be under assault?"

I was already saddened by death and dying around the globe: countries were at war inside their own borders, women and girls were captured and raped, and abject poverty prevailed in too many places. But an attack on America! This was too shocking to contemplate. I felt isolated and frightened.

Suddenly there was a ping in my brain. (Quite possibly my grandmother again!) "You can sit there yelling or you can do something about it!"

Who, me? Fix war and terrorism and other tragedies? Yeah, right. Who was this voice kidding?

"Do something with other women to carve a path to peace." That was it. Short and succinct.

"That's all very well," my brain argued, "but there are dozens of organizations already focused on that!" (The insecure part of my brain was determined to take over.)

"But your concept will be new and different from the others." Oh, all right then.

The thoughts kept thumping and wouldn't let me go. I started making notes. I would establish an organization led by women. An organization that would promote women at global decision-making tables; that would recognize that women need to stand up, speak out about peace and be heard; that women must be recognized for their leadership skills for the future of our planet.

The faces of many of my female friends in San Diego started to swarm my head. Staunch friends who were lawyers, accountants, activists, community organizers; the list kept growing. I wrote down their names. Then a name for the organization flew into my head. Voices of Women. VOW for short. I even drew a stylized tree as a potential logo. There was no going back now!

I was miles away from my husband and friends. All I wanted to do was get home. But how? President George W. Bush had grounded all flights across the country. Seattle is 1255 miles by road from San Diego, and I didn't have a rental car. Would I be stuck in Seattle for days, even weeks? Kim made calls to bus and train companies, but all were fully booked or not running. For four days we worked relentlessly to find transport home.

Out of the blue, my mentee Samuel phoned me. He knew I was in Seattle. After we discussed the tragedy, he said, "Hey, do you remember Megan, that girl I dated? Well, she's also stuck in Seattle, and she's managed to get the last rental car in town. Would you like to drive to San Diego with her?"

Would I ever! Megan and I connected, she picked me up, and we headed off on what we knew would be a long and tiring twenty-hour drive to San Diego. Near midnight, even though we'd both taken turns at the wheel, our eyes were closing. We checked into a very seedy motel. We tucked our wallets inside our clothing and snatched three hours of sleep. Then we got back on the road again and made it home to joyful reunions with loved ones.

Kim and I had a dinner party planned for the evening of my arrival. He thought I'd want to cancel it because of exhaustion. My reaction was the opposite: Fill the house with friends; they were exactly what we all needed. And so, we did. We were all in shock, as was the country and the world, and would stay that way for weeks and months to come as the grim details continued to assault us.

On that long drive home from Seattle, I couldn't get VOW out of my head. I'd been due to have lunch that day with four close female friends in San Diego. They went ahead without me, as they all needed to connect. I called them from the car and shared my ideas with them.

"I want to start a nonprofit for and about women and peace. Are you with me?"

They were, bless their hearts. But they had a lot of questions.

"How would we start? Where would we meet? How would VOW take shape? What would the goals be? Would you lead it?"

That was sufficient input to have my head reeling the rest of the way home.

Having a child is something new and beautiful. For those of us who can't have them, birthing a concept is beautiful too, and invigorating. VOW was already filling me with the promise and passion of a new venture that needed nurturing and feeding. It wouldn't all be peaches and cream; there was a hard slog ahead. But I had friends to help and remembered the adage: "One of us is never as good as all of us." We can do this! Bring on the work!

CHAPTER 30

The lady doth protest too much.
Hamlet

President Bush had been advising the country to stay away from all trade centers in case of another attack. Well, I've always been a bit of a rebel! I contacted a friend who ran her business in the San Diego Trade Center to ask her if I could rent a room for VOW's first meeting. She agreed, and on October 17, 2001, five weeks after 9/11, VOW was conceived!

Approximately thirty women attended that pivotal meeting. Several didn't appear because of the fear that the president had incited. After a welcome and introduction of the concept over coffee, we formed small groups and discussed questions: "How could women bring peace into policies?" "If more women step up into global leadership roles, what will their responsibilities be?" "How did we want our world to look, and how would VOW participate?"

The groups reported back. We took notes. We recruited women who were willing to serve as board members. A few months later, VOW was registered as a 501(c)3 charitable organization, and we were official!

A flurry of activity followed: Finding a space for the board to meet monthly. Drawing up guidelines. Considering the types of programs we wanted to present. Oh, and there was the matter of funding and how we would manage that. Not my favorite thing! Fortunately, financial experts had signed up for board positions. And the board had lots of questions. Will we invite men to join? Are there other organizations VOW should partner with? What if the public didn't support VOW? How would we get started? Well, I already had that one planned in my head.

We launched our first event at the theatre where I'd played Madame Arcati. The artistic director generously donated the space. A talented troupe of actors delivered poems and readings about war and peace, followed by a discussion. We filled the seats, and the audience was very appreciative. They welcomed a forum where they could air their fears and gain comfort, knowing they weren't alone. With this in mind, we staged a second event at the San Diego Repertory Theatre. The artistic director also donated their space. Once again, we invited actors to deliver historical words of battles and ensuing goodwill to a full house—another appreciative, absorbed audience.

With these successes under our belt, we moved on to create a relationship with the Joan B. Kroc Institute for Peace and Justice (IPJ) at the University of San Diego. The IPJ had been founded in 2000 at the behest of philanthropist Joan B. Kroc (widow of Ray Kroc) to pursue paths to peace. The mission: "Together with peacemakers, we develop powerful new approaches to end cycles of violence, while advancing that learning locally and globally." It spoke to us explicitly. A few of us had attended lectures and events at the IPJ that provided education and insights for VOW.

A small group of us approached the institute's director to ask if she would consider a partnership with VOW.

"Could we present a panel to discuss peace? Could we use their mailing list for invitations? Would they consider waiving the fee for the hire of the auditorium, as VOW didn't have any funding?"

The answer was a resounding "yes" to all. Exciting!

In early 2002, a VOW board member shared the stage with a *Los Angeles Times* reporter and the director of the IPJ. They discussed the effects of war on women and children, and if women could reshape the model of leadership. I moderated the panel, which was well received and sent us away thinking of grand schemes for peace. This event became the cornerstone of a partnership that would continue for several years through eighty-plus educational programs.

In 2003, the IPJ established the Women Peacemakers' Program (WPM), where annually, four women from all corners of the globe were selected to stay at the IPJ's hall of residence for two months to share stories and lectures about their work at the front lines of conflict, while gaining respite from the chaos in their countries.

For many, English was their second language, so I volunteered to coach them in public speaking to help them get over their nerves and feel comfortable addressing American audiences. We had a lot of fun doing this, and I was afforded the fabulous opportunity to learn from them. One of the WPMs from Africa asked if she could invite everyone to dance at the end of her presentation.

"Absolutely, yes," was my reply, and I also recommended, "Open your presentation in your native tongue to help you feel more comfortable."

Over the years, I have stayed in touch with several of the women. Dr. Rubina Feroze Bhatti from Pakistan returned a few years later to get her PhD at the University of San Diego. We reconnected and have remained friends despite the miles between us. Human rights lawyer Rutuparna Mohanty of India and I are still in touch. And I've enjoyed tea in Kenya with Wahu Kaara, a tireless activist for women in her country. Glenda Wildschut of South Africa and I share a love of rugby, and even though her country has great players, she always tells me, "My blood runs black" (for New Zealand's All Blacks). Rehana Hashmi of Pakistan gifted me a gorgeous shawl that I treasure to this day. And Ruth Buffalo, the first Native American peacemaker, reminds me of the need to honor the sacred spaces of the United States.

I relish the relationships with these women and have learned so much from and about them. Their resilience, strength, wisdom, and wit taught me about the tenacity and resolve innately embedded in women; that no matter where a woman comes from, she is determined to provide food and shelter for her children, to educate them, to stand up to autocracy and tyranny, and to fight for her rights and those of her fellow citizens. I draw strength from their stories:

"In 1989 we had to leave Afghanistan and went to Pakistan as refugees ... that became an opportunity ... I was 11 and I started teaching our landlady's children, so she waived the rent."

"In the late '70s, I became a survivor of sexual and gen-der-based violence."

"Peacemaking is mine to give, not yours to take."

"Our local governments are taking actions because of the work we are doing with police officers."

"Being a woman, I realized I should respond if there is some injustice, or some inequality …"

VOW continued to grow from strength to strength. My face and name were known in San Diego, and this garnered respect for Voices of Women. I had begun to recognize my leadership strengths and ability to communicate on a broad platform. I was finally "coming into myself," as the saying goes, and constantly invigorated by the opportunities to explore areas of life unknown to me before. My nurturing and mothering skills were focused in unexpected directions. And in parallel with VOW, I continued to operate Prisk Communication and travel across the country to deliver workshops and speeches. But there were more surprises in store!

CHAPTER 31

Nothing will come of nothing.
King Lear

I n 2008 I was offered an amazing opportunity. My mentee, Samuel, told me of his intention to fly to Peru to help rebuild a school in the small coastal town of Pisco that had been badly hit by a tsunami in 2007. He was joining the nonprofit organization Hands On Disaster Response and called me.

"Jenni, this is right up your alley! You'll get to visit a new country and help the people at the same time. Perhaps Kim would like to come too? Oh, and by the way, we'll be living in a communal building where you'll share a cramped bunk room with several others."

Despite a few misgivings, I was convinced, and invited Ann, who'd always wanted to visit Machu Picchu, just as I had. I had hoped Kim would join us, but he was involved in a project and couldn't leave town. Samuel was going to walk the Inca Trail, which sounded too strenuous for us, so Ann and I traveled comfortably by train from the capital Lima to Pisco.

Like most of us, I have ideas about a country I haven't visited, from books, television, and conversations. Peru was different from what I'd envisaged. Yes, there was abject poverty, but the people seemed happy, and the scenery was magnificent. The life that most Peruvians lead is simple and hard, yet the people are hospitable and personable. The terrain is varied, stretching from the Andean ranges to the Pacific Ocean. Pisco lies in the south, on the coast. It wasn't surprising that the town was damaged by the tsunami, generated by an 8.0 earthquake.

A team of ten of us from several different countries walked two miles to the school site each morning, carrying rudimentary tools. Under supervision by the local people, we built! I was assigned to soaking and carrying bricks to those constructing the walls. By the end of the week, I had embraced my nickname, "brick bitch." The days were hot and tiring, but the headmaster plied us with tons of water and good local food! And we got to meet some of the beautiful children, who were very excited about their new school.

The word "interesting" aptly describes the commune's thirty-plus residents. Every evening we sat together to eat and talk about the day's experiences. Some were rebuilding in the town. Many had stayed in communes before, as this was how they lived their lives—wandering the world and helping in disaster areas.

Words like smelly, sparse, scungy, and soiled describe the commune. We each slept fitfully in bunk rooms, with seven other people from a variety of countries. Many in our room spent the nights going to the loo with "Montezuma's revenge"! I was in a top bunk, about two feet from the ceiling that was crawling with spiders and other insects I didn't recognize. And it was cold. Our sleeping bags weren't nearly warm enough.

Breakfast was "grab what you can" from a selection of cereals, porridge, and bread. Showering was a luxury and a liability; there was plenty of hot water, but the shower door kept flying open. Evening meals around the campfire were fun. Everyone was invited to share a story from their life, and awards (a bottle of beer) were given for best story or other attributes. One night, the camp leader announced, "We're going to select the most beautiful person in this group." I looked around at the gorgeous young people, their cheeks glowing from the fire and the sun after their hard day's work, and made my choice on a piece of paper. To my utter surprise and embarrassment, I won the beer. I rode on that small accolade for weeks and am grateful to all those folks who didn't realize what a gift they'd given me.

It was the toilets that left the most indelible memory. At some stage during the week, each of us was assigned to toilet cleaning duty. We had all learned the phrase, "If it's yellow, let it mellow; if it's brown, flush it down."

The water in the toilets was already foul. I can remember Ann and I putting on rubber gloves, taking an enormous breath, and holding it until we'd scrubbed and cleaned whatever and wherever we could, and exited the room dry retching.

"There must be a place in heaven for us now," she said.

That was certainly our trip through hell.

At the end of the week, Ann and I embarked on the fascinating journey to Machu Picchu. First, a bus to Lima, then a flight to Cusco, an elegant "Imperial" city. Because it's in the middle of the mountains, you might think Machu Picchu is higher than Cusco, but it's not. Cusco's altitude reaches 3,399 meters/11,152 feet above sea level, while Machu Picchu's altitude is 2,430 meters/7,972 feet above sea level.

We were advised to adjust to the altitude by drinking coca leaf tea, which is the raw material used to make cocaine. Ann got very sick from it and thought she might die. I went into hyperactive mode and could have painted the town single-handedly. Despite all this, it helped us to adjust to the high elevation.

The train ride to Aguas Calientes from Cusco was delightful. Gorgeous mountainous scenery, comfortable seats, and excellent food. Aguas Calientes is at the bottom of the hill below Machu Picchu. We spent a rainy night in the charming village. The morning of our bus trip up the winding road to the mountain, it was still raining hard. We were starting to doubt we'd see anything of the view at the top. However, as we took our first step onto the site, the clouds lifted, the rain cleared, and the sun came out with a vengeance.

It's a breathtaking site and sight, with many dramatic spectacles to absorb. Lush green mountains and hills surround the perimeter of Machu Picchu, a fifteenth-century Inca citadel, located in the Eastern Cordillera of southern Peru. We ambled for hours and soaked up the history, the architecture, and the sun. It exceeded all our expectations.

"Tick that box," Ann said contentedly. "If I never travel anywhere else, I'm happy."

And so was I.

If you have a strong desire to visit a certain place in our world, start making plans now! Research it, discuss it, save for it, and make it happen. Travel is one of the most enlightening opportunities of our lives. During COVID-19, travel was greatly limited, and the world had to grasp the realization that we'd lost the gift of journeying to far-off lands. Experiencing a new culture, different terrain, unusual food, and unfamiliar people provide a new way of thinking. Politics take on a different perspective. And volunteering in a foreign country often provides free or cheap accommodation while affording different life perspectives.

CHAPTER 32

To unpathed waters, undreamed shores.
The Winter's Tale

My fifth decade was certainly a time of travel. Kim and I continued to make pilgrimages to New Zealand, and we also visited Vietnam with a couple of friends. What a fascinating, educational experience! I expected to stay in rudimentary accommodation, but I was so wrong. The hotels were five-star, very clean and comfortable, and the food was delicious. Perched on the edge of the South China Sea, bordered by Laos (and China) in the north and Cambodia in the south, this resilient country is known to the world because of *the war*. The Vietnamese people refer to it as "the American war." That made me smile.

In an air-conditioned van, we traveled from the north to the south, savoring every sight. We toured the ancient city of Hanoi; spent the night on a junk in Ha Long Bay, where we kayaked; biked around Da Nang; fell in love with the city of Hue, and ended our trip in Saigon (the name the Southern Vietnamese prefer that we call Ho Chi Minh City). We scrambled through narrow tunnels carved by the Viet Cong (Kim and I didn't get very far, stopped by claustrophobia and the fact that we got jammed in the tunnel because of our bulk, much to the amusement of our guide).

We ventured into Cambodia, which is also very beautiful but haunted by the horrendous killings of the Khmer Rouge. We stayed in Siem Reap, a charming city with comfortable accommodation, and drove to the formerly Hindu/now Buddhist temple, Angkor Wat. We arrived in time to watch the sunrise, when Kim exclaimed, "Hell, the mosquitoes get up early here!" They trailed us relentlessly as we explored the twelfth-century UNESCO World Heritage Site.

"Imagine what it would be like to build this, especially in the heat," Kim said, when he learned that the sandstone used to construct the national monument, at least five million tons' worth, had been carried from a quarry 25 miles away. The artwork is complex and fascinating, as are the trees whose vines wind through and up much of the temple buildings, choking many of them. If you've seen the movie *Tomb Raider*, you've seen those trees.

We discovered a complete change of scenery and geography the next year when we traveled to Iceland, the eighteenth largest island in the world. This striking, topologically diverse country offers amazing scenery, from grassy plains to steep mountain ranges, hot sulfur pools, and barren steppes. Icelanders are proud to be the frontrunner in the World Economic Forum's Global Gender Gap Index for nine years in a row because of their support of equality for women!

We love to travel and consequently have always attempted to invest our money wisely. Had we been blessed with children, our finances would have been largely spent on their upbringing and education. One of our greatest pleasures is helping our great-nieces and great-nephews with their university fees and book purchases.

In their first year, they get a sum to start them off, with the caveat that the amount will only be repeated in following years if they score grades of B+ and above! You can guess which one of us decided on this merit system! However, I believe it's helped them to strive.

Striving for status alone can become a burden. New Zealand is a predominantly socialist country where the credo of the "public good" is widespread. In San Diego, we were amazed at how important one's assets become, and how appearing "well-off" is a syndrome for some. The newest model of (expensive) car must sit in the garage; homes should look smart and upmarket; clothing should be of the latest style (also expensive). And paying off a mortgage is a rare thing. When a friend discovered that we don't have a mortgage, she gasped! "How on earth did you do that? I'll have a mortgage till I die!"

Seventh Decade

2009–2020

Becoming

REFLECTIONS

Sailing into the sixties! Hopefully into a scintillating decade for you—when you've put the hurt and the harm behind you to live the life you were meant to live.

"I've learned two important lessons in my life … I don't recall the first one; the second one is that I need to start writing things down."

"I don't know how to act my age; I've never been this age before."

"I'm going to retire and live off my savings … what I'll do the second week, I have no idea."

These clever quotations popped up on the internet. There wasn't an attribution, so thank you to whomever wrote them.

The brain starts to develop large holes through which information falls, often never to be found again. I loved it when someone said to me, "We've taken in so much data at this stage of our lives that our brains can only keep the important stuff." And don't feel bad when you find yourself standing in the middle of a room with absolutely no idea why you're there.

If you want to retire, do it! And if you're not ready yet, call it "refire" and rekindle your imagination and energy. Start a new enterprise. Rediscover old skills that you haven't used for years. Share your advice with young people. Become a mentor. Share your experiences! Teach your grandchildren.

Go to classes on topics you know nothing about. Take risks but also take care of your body; it's not as strong as it used to be. Treat yourself to outlandish things. Buy a piece of furniture for your home that you would never have considered buying twenty years ago. Hang out with young people. Give back to those who are struggling. Travel, sing, dance, paint, whatever takes your fancy. You've earned it. Love yourself more than you ever have.

Chapter 33

The day shall not be up so soon as I,
To try the fair adventure of tomorrow.
King John

Over the years, Kim has sprung some surprises on me. None more so than his gift for my 59th birthday (he likes to beat the decade). On a Friday in April 2009, out of the blue, he said: "We're going away for the weekend; go and pack a bag."

"Where are we going?"

"You'll find out in due course," he said with a wry smile.

"How will I know what to pack?"

"I'll tell you." That was a first. He didn't usually take a lot of interest in the clothes I took on a trip. But I did as I was told.

We loaded the car and headed to the airport. I still didn't know our destination. When you're a control freak, this is unnerving! As we approached the terminal, Kim let slip, "We're going to Las Vegas."

"Vegas!"

Both of us have an intense dislike of this garish city. Why the hell were we going there?

"There's something under your seat."

I pulled out a brochure. Facing me was a photo of four people "flying" toward the camera. Suspended in weightlessness.

"Oh my God," I screamed. "Am I going to fly in zero gravity?"

"Yes, you are," he replied with a grin from ear to ear. I could have ravaged him then and there on the freeway. I was still bursting with excitement at check-in. Las Vegas suddenly seemed like the perfect destination.

We arrived early at the Zero Gravity Corporation's office on a calm, clear Saturday morning. There was a buzz of excitement. I was trying to keep my enthusiasm at bay and be very nonchalant about the experience.

"My husband's flown thousands of parabolas in zero gravity; I know all about it," I thought. But I really didn't.

We donned navy blue flight suits, specially made to our size. Kim had sent my measurements and all other details to the office long before I knew anything about the surprise. Those of us who were flying were given a very bland but filling breakfast. I commented on it, and Kim replied: "If you do throw up, it's better for everyone around you if you barf plain food!"

We were given an extensive talk covering all safety procedures. Then we boarded the bus and headed for McCarran Airfield. Many in the group were couples, celebrating milestone occasions. How I wished Kim were with me, but as he said, "I can fly in zero-g with NASA anytime and not pay for the trip!"

We walked to the foot of the stairs of the 727 aircraft like astronauts strolling to their spacecraft. A uniformed attendant pinned badges upside down on our collars. That mystery would be solved later. The back of the plane had regular passenger seats. We took off our shoes and fastened our seat belts. The entire interior was padded, and all the windows covered. Kim had told me, "Seeing the horizon going either straight up or straight down is not a good sight for the brain."

In minutes, we were over open land and in safe flying territory. We were released from our seats and invited to take our places with our group. I was in the gold group, not because we were better or smarter, but because our socks were yellow! Twelve of us scrambled to the nose of the plane and sat on the floor, with our feet under guy ropes. The excitement and tension were palpable!

The flight instructor's voice was directive, "In just a few moments, we will enter Mars gravity. Release your feet slowly, lie face down, and do a push-up."

"He must be kidding," I thought. "I don't do push-ups!" But I did. And my feet came off the floor. Wow, that was impressive.

Mars gravity is 3/8th of Earth's gravity, so at that point I weighed much less than I usually do. "Might need to move to Mars," I thought.

Our next experience was Moon gravity, which is 1/6th of Earth's gravity. Now I weighed six times less than my normal weight! Definitely moving to the Moon now.

"Put one arm on the floor and raise your whole body in a push-up," came the instruction. And I did! Wow, wow! This was unbelievable!

The sound of the engines changed. The roar was louder; the pull was heavier. Our bodies were flattened into the floor of the plane.

"We're going for zero gravity. Release your foot bindings and fly!"

And there I was, flying in weightlessness. Wow, wow, wow!! It was incredible.

Kim had given me a few pointers about things to try. I attempted my first somersault. Head to my knees, knees to my chest, tip forward and roll. Priceless!

I lay on my belly, with my arms out in front of me and circumnavigated the walls of the cabin. Others in my group copied me.

"Where did you learn to do this?"

"From my husband; he's flown for hours in zero-g," I bragged.

I flew like superwoman. I giggled, smiled, and gasped at the experience. Thirteen parabolas of 25 seconds each. (A parabola starts with injection: as the aircraft travels upward, the pilots reduce engine speed and the zero-g aircraft follows a ballistic trajectory.) I could have kept going for days, weeks, months.

I floated upside down to a video camera attached to a wall of the plane, and pushed the record button. This would show the badge the right way up.

When the instructor called the final parabola, there was a series of loud groans throughout the plane. None of us wanted it to end. We all attempted to do something spectacular on the final free fall. And then it was over, and we were back in our seats for the return to the airfield. At the foot of the stairs, the captain turned our badges over and congratulated us. Back at the office, the champagne flowed and has never tasted so good.

Babbling like a child, I tried to explain the experience to Kim—then remembered I didn't have to. He knew. But what a gift he'd given me to experience a world beyond our world in an atmosphere like nothing I have known.

CHAPTER 34

All the world's a stage.
As You Like It

At the age of 61 I fulfilled a dream that I'd had since I was 16 (uncanny number reversal)! I was invited to play Katherina in a San Diego production of Shakespeare's *The Taming of the Shrew*. The cast was made up of seasoned actors, which I was not. And there was a new twist to the story: Petruchio, Kate's persistent admirer, was played by a woman! Sandra Ellis-Troy, an icon of the San Diego stage whom I'd long admired, would be my protagonist. Could I match her mastery and brilliance?

We ran for three weeks in a tired yet functional theatre in downtown San Diego. It was both a nerve-racking and exhilarating experience. Audiences applauded the gay theme and appreciated the different premise.

Learning lines has never been easy for me. I lose focus, and the rhythm of the words. Shakespeare's iambic pentameter has a sublime life of its own. Kate's final monologue of submission to Petruchio is 42 lines long. It was a hell of a summit to climb. I struggled to get it right. However, there was some leniency in that it's delivered solo, so there's no disruption to the other actors. One night, as I entered the dressing room after the final curtain, the cast was applauding and grinning at me.

"What's going on?" I asked innocently.

"You got the monologue right" came the joint reply! Geez, what a way to be remembered!

It turned out that there was a much safer theatre option for me—as a critic. I was invited to write reviews for an online magazine. When that entity closed, I started posting my reviews on Facebook under the nomenclature "Scene by Jenni Prisk."

Critics can be tough. I tend to err on the side of kindness. If I don't like the direction or the focus of an actor, I write sparingly of their work. I try to appreciate the overall effect and how the audience responds to the production. And in one or two cases, when I've really disliked the show, I haven't reviewed it at all! This might seem unprofessional; however, I appreciate the hard work and good intentions that go into producing a piece. Actors are poorly paid, they work long hours, spend much time away from their families, and are dedicated to their craft. I've always said that art documents history, and none more so than the foibles and fancies of humanity portrayed by actors on a stage.

The spoken word is so important for children as they learn. One of my greatest joys was to read weekly to first graders at a San Diego elementary school, which I did for ten years. Those little munchkins would sit (relatively) quietly on the carpet in front of me as we journeyed through *Winnie the Pooh* countless times, and the children made animal noises and answered questions about the stories. One day, a child in third grade came racing across the playground as I arrived at my classroom to read. Bursting with excitement, he said, "Mrs. Prisk, I have to tell you something. I'm reading to my little brother, and he loves it, and I am getting better and better at reading." That felt better than winning the lottery!

Despite my decision to leave the stage to those who could remember their lines, I caved when offered a part in *The Vagina Monologues*. The reason for caving? We would have our scripts at the podium! Eve Ensler wrote the *Monologues* in 1996 to amplify voices of women. In 1998, the *Monologues* became part of V Day, the fundraising movement dedicated to ending violence against women. The piece has been played around the world to great acclaim and to some scathing criticism.

"The Vagina Workshop Woman" role was assigned to me for the production at the San Diego Repertory Theatre (a homecoming of sorts). I had a blast. Each role is about ten minutes long, and in that time, each performer gives her all to her piece. Which I did! Using an affected British accent, I started with gentility and built to a promiscuous pinnacle as my character found her "happy bean" on the floor in a workshop surrounded by other women also finding theirs. Our production brought the house down and raised substantial funds.

CHAPTER 35

We know what we are, but know not what we may be.
Hamlet

During all these escapades, my business was booming. I was traveling across the US to provide workshops and to speak at conferences. My clients provided the opportunity to meet and work with some terrific people, many of whom I am in contact with today.

One experience that stands out was a series of trainings I provided for the US Navy SEALs (primary special operations force and a component of the Naval Special Warfare Command) in San Diego. The invitation requested that I deliver not only public speaking training, but also skills that would enable the men to professionally address senior members of the federal government. I introduced a 45-second impromptu speaking exercise by explaining that I would "model" the concept after one of the twelve in the room gave me a topic. Quick as a flash, one of the senior officers in the room called out: "Does size matter?"

The eyes of those magnificent fighting machines were all fixed on me. I couldn't fail. I delivered points about the size and scope of cities and governments, of populations, and of corporations. I got a standing ovation. And lots of laughter. I knew the path that that officer had wanted me to take. Instead, I gained their respect; much more important! Humor is a powerful way to diffuse nervousness or embarrassment, an aptitude I have encouraged in many women. When I left the final session, they lined up in the hallway and gave me the biggest, strongest hugs I've ever received.

Voices of Women continued to flourish and provide programs and insights into the world of women and their struggles globally. I felt strong. However, the drums of uncertainty still beat in my head: "Am I good enough?" "People have such faith in me, but should they?" "I'm not really as good as people tell me I am." Good old impostor syndrome again! I started an exercise. Whenever those negative thoughts came rushing in, I mentally told them to leave!

"Get the hell out of here! Piss off, I'm confident and I'm in charge here!"

And simple though it sounds, it began to work. I use this exercise to this day.

The Buddha said: "What you think, you become. What you feel, you attract. What you imagine, you create."

I'm very inclined to agree.

A San Diego woman of Ugandan descent attended one of VOW's programs and spoke with us afterwards. "There's a huge need in Kampala for education for women and girls; how to start a business, gaining confidence to speak up for themselves, and how to promote the livelihood of women in agriculture."

We formed a friendship with her, and a trip to Uganda began to take shape. Two of us (the other being the only male on our board) traveled with her to her country, stayed with her family, and spent the days exploring ways to assist these women who lived in poverty yet had the light of hope in their eyes. At the end of the week, we went on a safari. What an experience to ride in a jeep to see wildlife that approached our vehicle, as curious as we were. Sunsets and sunrises in Africa are like nothing on earth. I was hooked by the magic of the vast continent.

My interest in the lives and culture of African women led me to meet with an extraordinary group based in San Diego. All from East Africa, and all Muslim, they had formed an organization to perpetuate healthy living, camaraderie, and education for their youth and for themselves so that they could develop and sustain businesses. Through VOW, we spent many hours designing and delivering empowerment workshops, coaching individuals, and eating the delicious food they prepared in their center's kitchen. I'll always remember their ginger tea, its warmth and comfort at the end of a long day.

We laughed together a lot, too. The leader of the group has a particularly good sense of humor. One day, at the end of a session, she remarked, "Jenni and I have to leave now. We're going out to meet some guys for a glass of wine!"

Humor across cultures is one of the most effective connectors. It allows all involved to share common ground and grow relationships. Laughing together can lead to learning together and opens the doors of our hearts to acceptance and understanding.

The women explained Ramadan (the ninth month of the Islamic calendar, observed by Muslims worldwide as a month of fasting, prayer, reflection, and community) and its importance in their lives. Frequently when we were collaborating, they would leave to pray and return refreshed and ready to continue. They were quite comfortable with our eating while they fasted.

"I think I should celebrate Ramadan with you. I might lose some weight."

"But we eat all evening after sundown."

Clearly not a diet lifestyle!

CHAPTER 36

We are such stuff as dreams are made on …
The Tempest

B y this time, I'd joined the San Diego Rotary Club. Over the years, I'd given speeches at several Rotaries, and friends had suggested I might like to join. For whatever reason, I decided to wait till I was sixty to investigate the clubs. The San Diego Rotary Club is the fourth largest in the world, boasting a membership of 500+. Why not go for the gold? I did wonder if a club of that size would be welcoming and friendly. That thought soon went out the window.

"Jenni, welcome to our club. We're delighted to have you with us" was the refrain I heard all around the gathering. "Sit here with me, I'll introduce you to other Rotarians." The guest speaker was inspiring, and I was hooked. But I visited twice more to be sure. The same energy greeted me, so I joined. Frequently, women are put off joining Rotary as they consider it an all-male bastion. It used to be, but is no longer, and clubs are generously populated by women who regularly lead them.

There are several hoops to jump through before you truly earn your membership: showing up for events, volunteering for various club activities, joining committees. I didn't have to complete them all before I became a full member, as an opportunity landed in my lap.

A representative of the Old Globe Theatre was scheduled to be the speaker on one Thursday early in my membership. On the Tuesday of the same week, they cancelled. A board director approached me because he knew I was connected to the theatre in San Diego. "Could you find a replacement program?"

Immediately, I contacted Cygnet Theatre, as I know the fabulous artistic director, and asked if he would speak and bring a few actors to give us a preview of an upcoming show. He jumped at the chance, wowed the members, the actors outdid themselves, and I was "inducted" fully into Rotary the following month. It underlines that good old adage of "it's not what you know, but who."

One of the club's star events is Camp Enterprise. Eighty or more high school students are transported to the "woods" over a weekend to learn how to develop a business. Accommodated in cabins, the students work all day in teams, coached by Rotarians, and at night revel in some high jinks. Security is heavy; taking all those hormones to the hills is highly risky. What those young people learn over the two days is remarkable, and for some, it changes their lives forever. The adults are changed too. We're inspired by the grit and determination of the kids—some of them from homes where money was lacking, one who slept in their car, and others who'd experienced abuse.

A very important component that the club employed was not putting the kids' last names or their schools on their name tags. All were equal. All were included. I remember one remarkable young man in a group I facilitated. Another male student was exhausted and refused to participate. During the exercises, he laid his head on the table and wouldn't budge. The remarkable young man coaxed and coached him out of his funk to become a fully involved member of the team. He became the spokesperson for the group at the presentation competition! It blew us out of the water. Anything is possible when someone believes in you.

CHAPTER 37

Love all, trust a few, do wrong to none.
All's Well That Ends Well

By 2012, I had become a member-at-large (a term that's always made me smile, because originally it referred to someone on the run from the police) of the San Diego County Commission on the Status of Women and Girls (SDCCSWG). I was thrilled to be invited to join a delegation to the annual Commission on the Status of Women (CSW) at the United Nations in New York. The CSW is a functional commission of the United Nations Economic and Social Council, one of the main organs within the United Nations. CSW is the UN organ promoting gender equality and the empowerment of women. This was right in my wheelhouse. Thus far I've been to five of these exhilarating (and exhausting) meetings.

On average, 5,000–7,000 women (and many men) from around the globe assemble at the UN for two weeks of meetings on a wide variety of topics that impact women. The official meetings commence at 9 a.m. and conclude at 5 p.m. The unofficial meetings continue into the night over glasses of wine. Many allegiances and alliances are formed, which we each carry back to our respective cities and countries, filled with progressive ideas for our regions.

And, of course, one of the greatest delights of visiting New York was the opportunity to see some great theatre.

From 2015 to 2017, I chaired the SDCCSWG. It was invigorating to partner with twelve fine women, all dedicated to ensuring that women's rights were recognized in our fair city. We produced conferences and seminars, hosted guest speakers, spoke about the commission around the region and focused on homelessness, domestic violence, and human trafficking as our key issues.

While I was in my chair role, the Association of California Commissions for Women (ACCW) invited me to put my name forward as their president. I was voted in and spent two highly involved years meeting with women throughout California, learning about the status of women in our state and collaborating with other female-focused organizations. My dreams of promoting the empowerment of women were coming true.

One of my greatest pleasures during this decade was to emcee the San Diego County Women's Hall of Fame. Five, and sometimes six, amazing women who are trailblazers or simply kick-ass in their fields are inducted by a judge in front of a large audience. In my humble opinion, this should take place in every city in every state in every country. The more we honor women, the more we honor our nations and our future. Just sayin'.

All of us on the VOW board attended educational lectures and presentations that focused on women and girls, and my dear friend Carol brought a wonderful story to a board meeting. She'd been at the IPJ and heard from the founder of a girls' school in Laikipia County near Nanyuki, Kenya. Jason Doherty was an alumnus of the University of San Diego and had long harbored a wish to provide education for girls in a country that he loved and knew was hurting for lack of good facilities and teachers. He and his wife Jenni (not a typo) founded The Daraja Academy to provide a haven for girls whose families couldn't afford the fees for the "regular" schools in Kenya.

We all met Jason and Jenni. After extensive conversations, board member Nadine and I offered to design a course in business development and teach it at the school. We were accepted. A thrilling opportunity.

I can still remember the very bumpy, very dusty ride in the van from Nanyuki to Laikipia. To get to Nanyuki, we had flown from Nairobi, passing over the Kibera slums, a sight I will never forget. From the warmth and comfort of our plane, we looked down at the countless acres of decay, detritus, and desolation that is home to hundreds of thousands of people. "This will help us remember how fortunate we are," Nadine whispered to me.

Daraja appeared out of nowhere. A rickety gate and a friendly gatekeeper were the only barriers to the outside world for some forty girls. Nadine and I arrived during the school holidays; however, the seniors who wanted to learn about business had stayed behind to work with us. We were met with joyful greetings of "Jambo," hearty hugs, and the biggest smiles

with the whitest teeth! The girls showed us to our accommodation. A small, comfortable, circular thatched hut (banda)
with two bunks, a tiny bathroom, and a tiny sitting area. The
mzungus had landed!

We lined up each morning for a breakfast of beans and an
egg. Lunch was very simple, perhaps a small piece of chicken.
And dinner was more beans with rice. The cooks were amazing.
They pulled dishes for 25 of us out of a hat. We chose not to
shower at the banda, as the water ran dark brown. We used to
sniff each other every morning to make sure we'd done our best
to clean all body parts!

The girls were motivated to learn how to develop a business.
Their concentration and commitment were palpable. They
formed teams, and as each project developed, they became
more excited about the opportunities a business could have for
them when they left Daraja. Nadine, who is an accomplished
artist, taught them how to design their logos, and I helped
them with their business strategy and public speaking skills.

The girls presented their concepts to the teachers and
founders of the school. They quite overwhelmed us with their
poise and confidence.

Nadine and I left the school and the girls with much sadness.
However, we embarked on a three-day safari through the Great
Rift Valley where we visited with the Masai Mara tribes and
witnessed some incredible animal activities. Once again, the
magic of Africa assailed my senses and I yearn to return.

CHAPTER 38

O this learning, what a thing it is!
Taming of the Shrew

In 2015, I was afforded a unique opportunity—to attend a course on international relations at Oxford University in England! The San Diego State University College of Extended Studies has an Oxford Study Abroad Programme (OSAP). I had collaborated with one of the lecturers while teaching at The Hansen Institute at San Diego State University. He invited me to join the 2015 cohort, so after much discussion with Kim, I did!

When choosing your life partner, be sure this person has your interests at heart and is willing to respect your dreams and ambitions. They may not always want to join you. However, if they are comfortable with your adventures, taken alone or with others, then you've struck gold! Kim has always had my back. He exemplifies a reading at our wedding from *The Prophet* by Kahlil Gibran, "And stand together yet not too near together:

For the pillars of the temple stand apart, And the oak tree and the cypress grow not in each other's shadow." Thanks, big guy!

I departed for the hallowed town of Oxford in late December 2015 and returned in early January 2016. Not the warmest time to visit England; however, our enthusiasm and excitement kept us cozy. I was the oldest (by far) of the group of twenty students, but they never let that get in the way and neither did I. We were lectured on US-UK relations in small cold classrooms and in elegant university lecture halls.

Our accommodation was sparse, but comfortable, with a table in each room for study. And study we did. There were exams to sit (horrors!) and deadlines to meet. And when time permitted, opportunities to stroll through the streets of this twelfth-century "city of dreaming spires" and soak up the history and architecture.

Oxford is ancient and graceful, but it hosts some wild bars and nightclubs, as we found out on New Year's Eve. We danced and partied into the wee small hours at several venues and welcomed 2016 in bleary style the next morning. I think I may have danced harder and longer than some of my younger counterparts if the sore calf muscles I had the next day were any indication.

The pressure for me was high when I sat the final exam. The students were used to the stress of intensive study and handled it well. I was in a lather when we received our papers. Had I reviewed the right stuff? Would this whole course be a waste of time? Would I be a failure? (Those darned messages again.)

When I first read the paper, nothing seemed to make sense, until I read it again, and again, and then I got it! I wrote for the entire time, handed the paper in with much relief, and was beyond thrilled to receive an A!

Before I left for Oxford, we'd made a major decision at VOW. Several of the directors were retiring from the board due to ill health in themselves or in their families. We didn't have the heft to continue as an organization. It was painful and painstaking to dismantle the nonprofit we had loved. Many of my feelings of inadequacy returned. Is this my fault? Would it have survived longer with different leadership? Should we have merged with another similar organization?

Every founder has these thoughts and feelings. But the time had come to close the doors, distribute the remaining funds to charities, and kiss VOW goodbye. We promised to stay in touch, and we have. We still have reunions. This is possible when there are no recriminations or finger-pointing.

CHAPTER 39

Speak the speech, I pray you ...
Hamlet

I n 2016, one of the board directors and I got together to
discuss a new idea. She has skills and talents as a doc-
umentary producer; I'd always harbored the idea that we
should be concentrating on the actual voices of women, so
iVOW (www.voicesofwomen.org) was born!

We strategized the podcast to feature women's voices
telling the stories of their roles in marginalized commu-
nities and male-dominated professions. We were fortunate to have many good connections throughout the San
Diego region. We started by interviewing the women
peacemakers at the IPJ, who enriched our lives with their
stories of struggle and strength. We interviewed four
California politicians who gave us great insights into
their road to leadership.

One of the women, Congresswoman Susan Davis (now retired), who served for twenty years in the 53rd Congressional District, told a humorous yet stinging story.

"When I was first elected to Congress, my husband was asked (in Washington, DC) by a reporter: 'Sir, are you the new member of the House?' When my husband said no, the reporter didn't even glance at me!"

Our interviews with inmates at Las Colinas women's prison were enlightening and encouraging. This groundbreaking penitentiary provides the women with career training so that when they're discharged, they have a new start to life.

One of the women inspired us by saying: "How you treat yourself is how other people will treat you. It's important that women have a voice, and potential; we're not hopeless. It's not all dark in here; the staff really respect us."

We talked with women in the military, from Syria, with law officers, and continued to interview the women peacemakers annually. We engaged an intern, Zack, and he and I continue to search for interviewees. This is something I plan to operate until I run out of breath, although COVID has slowed us down.

Zack became my associate at Prisk Communication for a year. I was starting to get tired of crisscrossing the country for work and needed an assistant. Zack was interested at that stage in getting into a communications role like mine, so the match was perfect. My clients loved him and welcomed him with enthusiasm. We had fun sharing the instruction and he provided the much-needed millennial approach for many of the participants.

There's a great balance to be had between a baby boomer and a millennial. You *can* teach an old dog new tricks! Zack and I discussed the possibility of his taking over the business. We decided that my clients with whom I'd built a relationship over many years would find him young (he was 23) and lacking in the full experience required to take over the leadership of Prisk Communication. Eventually, Zack's interests began to veer in the direction of marketing and social media, so we parted ways amicably and remain very close friends to this day.

And by this time, Kim and I had an exciting project in the works.

CHAPTER 40

No legacy is so rich as honesty.
All's Well That Ends Well

"TED Talks" are familiar words. They pop up everywhere. Some terrific folks have presented some terrific discourses. I've been fortunate to deliver one and emcee two. An innovative businesswoman in San Diego had a great idea—to start SUE (Successful, Unstoppable, Empowering) Talks by and about women. (I'm pleased to say that men are now speaking at these events too!)

I was invited to deliver a twelve-minute presentation that we called "Think Outside Your Brain." The idea was to present business advice in parallel with personal stories. I made the bold decision to talk about my father. It was time. The speech took some time to write, and I was worried as I had to memorize it, something I never do at the podium. My advice to my speech clients has always been that "Only actors memorize!"

172

I've always found it's best to be prepared with solid bullets that link to each other so that the speaker sounds spontaneous.

The speech was finally ready. Kim and I drove to Costa Mesa, north of San Diego (where I'd sat my LTCL exam), for the event. The speeches were delivered at a dinner. Five of us spoke. All moving stories. I was welcomed onto the stage with rousing music. The lights lowered. A spotlight shone on me, and I began. "My father was a pedophile," and it was out. I'd said it in public. I'd freed myself. I'd put the blame squarely on him and taken it away from me. Wow, what a feeling. In that speech I also included two promises to myself. "I will meet Michelle Obama, and I will be on a show with Oprah." Neither has happened yet, but I'm still hoping!!

That speech was the catharsis that began my healing journey. I was no longer ashamed of the secrets I'd hidden. I wasn't ostracized for sharing them. In fact, I was applauded, long and loud, for letting them out. My SUE Talk is on YouTube and occasionally I'll play it just to remind myself of the promises I made to myself. Haven't fulfilled them all yet, but I will sure try.

I implore you to share any burden you carry that holds you back from reaching your full potential. I got professional help. I continue to take the medication that works miracles for me. And I find myself embarking on adventures and journeys that I once would have thought impossible. Now that my brain is clear, my body can proceed. And my purpose on this planet has become my passion. (Oh, and by the way, I've sent a copy of this book to Michelle and Oprah!)

CHAPTER 41

For here, I hope, begins our lasting joy.
Henry VI, Part 3

I n 2016, we went on the trip of a lifetime. To Antarctica! It had been on our bucket list forever, as New Zealand is only three thousand miles from the cold continent. Kim's school friend and my work colleague, Craig, rang us out of the blue one evening from Sydney. I heard Kim's side of the conversation: "Yep, we have some free time in March. Yep, yep, both of us. Holy crap, Antarctica!" Hearing that word, I knew I'd cancel a meeting with Oprah to go there.

A shipping company was offering a trip in late March, across the Drake Passage to the icy peninsula. There would be ten in our group and a total of seventy on board. This was appealing, as we'd never wanted to make the trip on a cruise ship with thousands. The advantage of the smaller ship meant that we could go ashore frequently. Only a hundred people at a time can walk on the pristine land.

We weren't kitted out in San Diego for below-freezing temperatures, so had a frantic shopping trip where we bought thermal underwear (if you want to look sexy, don't wear these), heavy waterproof jackets, gloves, hats, socks, and boots.

We flew to South America and spent a couple of days in exciting Buenos Aires. Then to Ushuaia, the southernmost tip of the continent, from where the ship departed. It was an exhilarating feeling as the ship weighed anchor and embarked on the 48-hour, 600-mile journey across the Drake Passage, one of the roughest crossings in the world. We took seasickness prevention, but that wasn't enough for some on board, who suffered from the high waves and turbulent seas. Mealtimes were a riot, trying to serve ourselves from the buffets while clinging to poles and avoiding throwing our meals all over someone else. At times, the waves towered above us as we sat and ate.

Naturalists on board gave presentations about the flora and fauna we would see on the peninsula. Kim was unexpectedly invited to give his presentation on "Taking Your Lungs to the Moon." Now, he knows that the title of one of my presentations is "Seize the Day, not the Podium." On the day he spoke, he didn't dare let go of the podium. He would have slithered his way across the lounge and crashed into the windows!

We knew we'd arrived in the waters of the white continent when the ship became calm and all was quiet. In the dark of morning, we peered through our porthole and saw icebergs everywhere. We had made it to the bottom of the world! These quotes say it better than I can:

"If Antarctica were music, it would be Mozart. Art, and it would be Michelangelo. Literature, and it would be Shakespeare. And yet it is something even greater; the only place on earth that is still as it should be. May we never tame it."—Andrew Denton

"Antarctica still remains a remote, lonely and desolate continent. A place where it's possible to see the splendors and immensities of the natural world at its most dramatic and, what's more, witness them almost exactly as they were, long, long before human beings ever arrived on the surface of this planet. Long may it remain so."—Sir David Attenborough

Over the next five days, we climbed onto Zodiac boats and zoomed to various inlets and bays on the Antarctic peninsula. Before we left the ship, we disinfected our boots so as not to take any diseases onto the land. We stood in freezing cold, under a glaring sun, staring at miles of white slopes, rocky mountains, glacial faces, icy cold water, and thousands of penguins. The penguins weren't afraid of us; they would wander right up to our feet and stand and stare, then wander off again. Seals and whales were abundant in the icy waters. It was beyond magic.

And we did the "polar plunge." Kim was very keen, as were the rest of the males in our party. We put on swimsuits under our thermal underwear. I was the only one of the "mature" women who decided to strip off on the "beach" with a fearsome windchill factor and run like hell into the freezing water. All I could hear as I ran down the beach was "f—k, f—k, f—k," and realized later it was me. Kim fell backwards into the water ahead of me. I reached him and dunked down until my shoulders and the bottom of my hair were wet, then shot up again, ready to run ashore. We were met by a crew member holding a giant towel and a very large vodka, which I can still taste and feel to this day!

There are days when I speak to my 90-year-old self to ask her how I'm doing in life, and if she wants me to change course or follow a different path. I can tell you that her reply on that day was "Attagirl!"

CHAPTER 42

When I was at home I was in a better place.
As You Like It

Now it was time for an exciting new project. In 2000, when we were visiting our family in New Zealand, we spent some time in the Bay of Islands. This gorgeous spot on the east coast of the North Island is surrounded by bush, rivers, beaches, and lush greenery, and is a major center for kiwifruit. We fell in love with the area, looked at each other, and said, "We could retire here."

Most of our family thought that if we did ever return to New Zealand, we'd settle in the South Island where we met. But it's much colder there. We'd become wimps after the gorgeous weather in San Diego. The north of New Zealand is subtropical, often referred to as the "winterless north." Although it does rain—a lot!

On the four-hour drive back to Auckland airport, we discussed the prospect. It was still very appealing. When we arrived at the airport, we couldn't find any signs for the rental car drop-off. Being a male, Kim wouldn't ask for directions, and the car didn't have a GPS.

"Pull over to the curb and I'll go to the information desk," I demanded.

There was a gentleman standing at the desk. He looked at me and I at him. We smiled, and then:

"Jenni?"

"Gavin?"

Gavin had been the Trade Consul for New Zealand in Los Angeles at the time I was the Chair of the San Diego New Zealand Business Association, back in the '80s. We hadn't seen each other since.

"What are you doing in New Zealand?"

"Visiting family," I replied. "What are *you* doing?"

"Settling a few things in New Zealand. I'm now married to a woman from the Czech Republic and am living there. Do you like Northland?"

"We love it! We think we might retire there."

"I own almost an acre of sloping land with water views that I'm in the process of selling. I don't suppose you'd be interested?"

It was as though I'd entered a time warp, and this wasn't really happening! We quickly exchanged business cards, I got directions to the drop-off, and farewelled Gavin.

When I returned to the car, I gave Kim the directions and casually said, "Oh, and I might have a piece of land for us!"

We talked about the prospect all the way back to San Diego. And were reminded of the adage: "It's not what you know, it's who!"

Soon after our return, and the exchange of many messages and photos, Kim flew back to New Zealand to view the property. He visited several other properties for sale, and when he returned to "the hill," decided it was the one. In an emotional phone call to me, I asked him, "Could you live there?"

His answer was a resounding "yes," so the property became ours.

Fast forward to 2017, the year of the build. We researched New Zealand architects on the internet, and then Kim flew down to interview eight of them. We chose the one who mentioned that he'd completed several projects with a reputable builder, and would Kim like to meet him? He did, and we selected him too.

Designing and building a house on the other side of the world is fraught with challenges. You can't visit the site regularly. Kim flew down when we broke ground on the land, which meant cutting away tons of dirt to flatten the section. He was fascinated by the process, like a kid playing with trucks. I received lots of photos and videos.

Then we had to choose floor materials, wall paint, fittings for the inside and out, faucets and sinks and basins, and on and on the list went. We made our selections in a week in New Zealand and hoped they were the right ones. They were.

In October 2018, we took possession of our new home. It was a dream come true. We'd shipped a container of some of our furniture from San Diego. It was pleasing to put familiar pieces in their new places. We might be retiring, but they weren't!

Speaking of retirement, Kim had asked me one day, "You're always so busy. How do you think I should fill my retirement hours?"

"With woodwork," I said. "You're good at it," referring to one table he'd built.

"I'll think about it," he replied.

Well, think about it he did, and today we have a house filled with beautiful pieces he's designed and built.

Retirement can be a distressing time for relationships. It's a whole new way of life, often accompanied by a sense of worthlessness and lethargy. As we age, it's important to have conversations about retirement activities. "What have you always wanted to do but couldn't while you were working?" "Do you have any goals for the next few years?" "Now that you're no longer working, which of your skills could you utilize in a different setting?" The more you talk, the saner you'll stay!

So, our plan was to live six months in San Diego and six months in Aotearoa—New Zealand. We achieved that rhythm once, then COVID-19 consumed the world. We were required to stay in New Zealand for two-plus years. No complaints, though! It's a beautiful country, and we have family scattered across both islands.

We quickly made friends in the neighborhood by inviting them all over for a glass the first week we moved in! They'd watched the house being built, so were dying to see inside.

I started art classes, something I'd thought about for years and never had the time to do. I enjoy painting the faces of feisty women. Why is that not surprising!

I've joined the Kerikeri Rotary Club. Its membership is small—a vast difference from the San Diego Rotary—but the energy and enthusiasm for service is built from the same stuff. I'm a member of Global Women NZ, an organization founded by New Zealand's first female prime minister, Dame Jenny Shipley. Comprised of women in leadership roles throughout the country, they constantly inspire me. In partnership with Dame Jenny and an exceptional wahine Maori friend, we are mobilizing meetings with Maori women in the north to support and advance their leadership.

And I've come home. Home to the land, home to the people, home to myself. While I will always love San Diego and all it gave us over forty years, New Zealand is my birthplace. I've always respected the privilege of being a Kiwi. Deeply rooted in "the land of the long white cloud" (Aotearoa), the country has steadied me, balanced me, and called me back. It's where I hope to grow very old, and die.

While I understand that reaching seventy is distressing for some people, for me it has been freeing. The years have peeled away the layers of self-doubt and guilt and replaced them with serenity and peace. And those seven decades are all mine. They started with a blank page on which to write. Have I always written well? No way! Have I made mistakes? You bet! Am I sorry? No! Because this life is mine. Just as yours is yours. You came here with a purpose. You have seventy years (and I hope more) to live, love, and be loved. You deserve the riches and rewards. You deserve tranquility from your fulfilled dreams and desires. You deserve to be seen, heard, and recognized! Whoever you are, wherever you are, whatever your calling, stand in your spotlight and live life fully!

EPILOGUE

So, I made it to my seventies. I celebrated my birthday in my beloved native land, surrounded by family and friends from San Diego and from our new neighborhood. They voiced expressions of love and gratitude for me. And I heard them. And absorbed them.

Body parts are starting to hurt a bit now, especially in the mornings. I brush that off by taking a long walk (or a couple of Ibuprofen)! I feed carrots to the local horses who nuzzle me and search my pockets. I walk through a beautiful woodland so I can watch dogs romp among the trees. I worry less and live more. In the beauty of nature.

I take a nap when I'm tired. And read some fascinating books. I've made many new friends. The local Rotary Club made me an honorary member. I'm coaching Maori women to speak up and be heard. I'm going to dance classes to learn rumba and samba and the cha-cha. I've stayed in touch with all my business colleagues and clients in San Diego to provide coaching and training on Zoom. And, I've been attending workshops on theater directing!

Kim and I love to entertain and fill our house with guests. We travel throughout New Zealand to be inspired by the sights of this gorgeous country. I've had my cataracts removed, so I no longer need glasses. (One benefit of ageing!) And I've written a book!

Plans for the future? I'd like to write books for children. And start a Socrates Café (gatherings where people from different backgrounds get together and exchange philosophical perspectives based on their experiences). I've yet to see the pyramids and other amazing sights on our beautiful planet. And I hope always to encourage and support women everywhere.

If I get frustrated or concerned, I close my eyes and imagine I'm sitting on a rock on the moon staring back at our magnificent blue marble. I try to identify my country, then my home, and then myself. All have disappeared beneath the clouds that swirl above our planet. My troubles diminish as I realize that I'm part of something spectacular; that I'm made from the same stuff as the stars; that for a brief moment in time I've had the privilege of living fully on this earth.

I hope I have at least twenty more years to live. But if I don't, I'll leave this world a happy, fulfilled woman. Who learned to love herself. And to stand in her spotlight.

ABOUT THE AUTHOR

Jenni Prisk was born and raised in New Zealand. In 1983, she and her husband moved to San Diego, California, where they have lived for almost forty years. She has an LTCL in Speech and Drama from Trinity College, London. Jenni founded award-winning Prisk Communication to provide public speaking and communication skills throughout the United States and internationally. She chaired the San Diego County Commission on the Status of Women and Girls from 2015–2017. Jenni served as President of the Association of California Commissions on the Status of Women (ACCW) from 2016–2018 and as an Ambassador for United State of Women (USOW). Jenni founded and hosts iVOW, a podcast program that features the voices of marginalized women (www.voicesofwomen.org).

She has served as an advisory member of the Women Peacemakers' Program at the Institute for Peace & Justice at the University of San Diego, and has worked extensively to uplift refugee women. Jenni is a founding committee member of the San Diego Workplace Equity Initiative and a member of Global Women NZ. She continues her passion for theatre as a critic. Jenni loves travel, gardening, walking, and painting, and oscillating life between San Diego and the Bay of Islands, New Zealand.

Please click on the following links to see and hear Jenni Prisk speak:

https://www.youtube.com/watch?v=F-Q6gdlyzN8
https://www.youtube.com/watch?v=tTADRnPO7q4
https://www.youtube.com/watch?v=iPcDHf07qOg

Twitter: https://twitter.com/jenniprisk; @jenniprisk
LinkedIn: https://www.linkedin.com/in/jenniprisk/

My Request to You

Most women don't throw themselves "out there" with requests to their readers. However, as you've just finished reading my book, you'll know that I encourage this! So, here's my request to you: if you know of a company, organization, nonprofit, university—you get the picture—anywhere on the planet who would like me to speak about my experiences, please have them contact me at jenni@prisk.com

My goal is to uplift, empower, and embolden everyone to be their best! To help them see their unique place in the world! To show them that they can overcome anything to succeed. To encourage them to go for gold and achieve their dreams.

Thank you!

ADDENDUM

Following are a few articles I have written over the years:

Embracing Age Over Ageism

Originally published in *Forbes*, April 22, 2019
Reprinted with permission

Since I recently turned 70, I find myself reviewing my life. Was I really a baby, then a toddler, a child, a teenager, and ultimately a woman? Where did those seven decades go? Who am I and what have I learned? How much of the "me" today was forming in the "me" of yesterday? How have my experiences shaped what I have to give and share?

As a young girl, I wrote short plays and performed them for my long-suffering parents. As a diffident, abused teenager I took to the stage in high school to escape from the real world. At 21, I left my native country of New Zealand on a ship and toured England and Europe, where I played, worked, and made discoveries for three years. When I turned 40, I started my speaking and training business. In my fifties, I founded a nonprofit that empowered women and girls. In my sixth decade, I chaired commissions for women both locally and statewide. Now at 70, I'm finding inner peace, self-knowledge, and unexpected vigor! I'm now a theatre critic. I travel extensively and live in two countries. I'm still a speech coach, and my greatest passion is empowering women to speak up and be heard.

Why am I sharing all this with you? I have experiences to pass on to others, especially women. You do, too. *You* have lived a life that is full and rich with adventures and wisdom. Women of your own decade and younger women yearn to learn from you. Your influence is invaluable. And if you need a reminder, here they are:

Your Education

You may have a science degree or a marketing degree or a degree in nursing, or you're a doctor, lecturer, teacher, or business owner. Do you share these tangible proficiencies with the younger ones in your life? Chances are they don't even know you have letters after your name, nor do they understand the struggles you overcame to stand at the top of your field.

Do they know that you shared campus life, late nights, early mornings, crammed for finals, shared copious coffee klatches, and the thrill (or despair) of exam results?

Perhaps you never had those opportunities. Maybe you learned by doing and found growth without a degree. (That was *my* path.) Your insight is equally valid and worthy of sharing. Does your circle know about the nights you spent poring over bills, the extra shifts you had to pick up to support your family, or that you combed through the newspaper searching for opportunities as you rode the bus to work?

No matter how you found self-betterment, you have an indisputable education. And you should be proud. What a world of mentoring you can provide! Tell the people in your life about your experiences—hardships and triumphs alike.

Uplift, teach, and support the women in your life by sharing the lessons you've learned.

Your Resilience

There's not a woman reading this who hasn't been put down, fallen over, cried over the dishes, been hurt, felt overlooked, been dropped, drunk too much, or called out to the universe about her place in it. And look where you are today! You are strong; you are resilient; you are unbreakable. Those gentle lines around your eyes and mouth have been earned from those years of living, learning, and laughing. Without knowing it, you share the wisdom you've gained with those who matter to you as you guide them through their growth pangs. You became an icon in their eyes because you lived, lost, and won gracefully. Never forget what you are to others: a role model, a mentor, a confidant, a friend. Even in small ways we impact and improve the lives of those around us by letting them know how human we are. If a woman is losing her grip on hope, don't offer sympathy. Grab her hand and pull her up. When a woman expresses self-doubt, take her to a mirror and let her see how amazing she is. If she's uncertain of her path, walk some of it with her.

Your Voice

One of the glorious things about ageing is that we become more comfortable speaking up. We have learned how to say things that matter and to fight for the things that matter more. I've always been a volunteer, but now I'm doing more work in the community and for women than I've done in years. Just last year I became an Ambassador for the United State of Women.

Do you watch or read the news and seethe? Do you grieve about the plight of girls around the globe who cannot get an education? Do you see female politicians being slandered for their forthright opinions? Do you get mad when the lawmakers want to take away your rights? You can do something about these things. You can write letters to your newspaper! You can talk it up on social media! You can share your thoughts with friends and colleagues! You can join (or found) an organization that will utilize your skills and your wisdom! You have a lifetime of knowledge and understanding to share.

We need to be mindful of age discrimination and remember what we can learn from the women who have been fighting to secure our rights for generations. Let's collectively reject ageism. This "cult" is an unhealthy scourge that suppresses the wealth of talent that older (people) women possess. The World Health Organization (WHO) in 2018 released this statement: Between 2015 and 2050, the proportion of the world's population over 60 years will nearly double from 12% to 22%. The rest of the population had better get used to us; we're not going away anytime soon!

So, get together with the WAGs (Women Ageing Gracefully) in your neighborhood or place of business, talk up your talents, share your successes, and celebrate your accolades. Form an organization with the goal of imparting your knowledge and life experiences to those who will benefit. You are a presence, and you matter! In the words of our former First Lady, Michelle Obama, "You have become!"

Mark My Words: There Is Power In Your Voice

Originally published in *Forbes*, February 26, 2020
Reprinted with permission

When a baby is born, everyone waits anxiously for that first cry, and to hear a voice that announces the child's presence on our planet.

We are unique in the animal kingdom in that we communicate verbally. Scientists are not sure when humans first spoke, but they speculate that language began two million years ago from the need to communicate while making tools. Today, there are roughly 6,500 languages spoken globally.

We tend to take our voices for granted. We open our mouths and words flow forth. When used wisely and appropriately, the voice can be one of the most powerful instruments in the human body. Swedish Musicologist Johan Sundberg once said: "The human voice has been called 'the mirror to our soul.'" He was referring to singing, but this statement also applies to the speaking voice. We transmit our feelings, emotions, ideas, wishes, in fact, everything through this singular, amazing instrument.

Women's voices are like violins in an orchestra; men's voices are the cellos. Because the female voice often registers at a higher tone than the male's, women can be overlooked, unheard, or ignored. If a woman's voice is "shrill," she is labeled as a whiner (or worse) and can be the recipient of unfair criticism and disparagement. If a woman is soft-spoken, she is written off as weak, submissive, or incapable.

I've spent 30 years as a voice coach, and in that time I've learned a great deal about the ways women compensate for vocal scrutiny. For example, if a woman wore braces on her teeth when she was young, the years she spent trying to hide them created a tight-lipped speech pattern. When the air cannot escape the mouth through open articulation, it settles at the back of the throat and constricts the voice. Many women's voices trail off at the end of phrases because of uncertainty about the receipt of their message. A deep inhaled breath before speaking will prevent this from occurring, as the breath will carry the message with strength through to its conclusion.

When a woman speaks quickly without pausing, using fillers to sustain momentum, her message can become confusing. Learning to slow her pace, to inhale while speaking, and to insert pauses, will give her voice more gravitas.

We can all regularly monitor our voices to ensure that we always sound strong and confident. When you want to hear the voice that emanates from your person—the voice that everyone else hears—cup your hands behind your ears (do not do this while driving!), gently bend the helix (ear flap) forward, bring your elbows together in front of you and imagine that you are greeting a friend: "Hello, how are you? It's good to see you." How do you sound? Strong, confident, assured, and positive, or scratchy, high-pitched, and tight, perhaps with nasal overtones?

Practicing a few exercises will ensure that our messages are heard. The power and pattern of our breathing are paramount. With your lips closed, inhale deeply through your nose. Exhale slowly through your mouth. Take a break and repeat three times (you will overventilate if you do too many, and possibly lose your balance).

Now, pick up something to read. Stand up (our projection is 25% better when we are on our feet because the diaphragm is expanded), inhale, and read a line or two while exhaling. Repeat, then cup your hands and listen to your voice. Has it changed? Is it more mellow? If not, inhale deeply through your mouth, then exhale on a continuous succession of "HAs" from your diaphragm and listen again.

The pace at which we speak is vitally important. When we rush our dialogue, we insert fillers, often trail off at the end of sentences, and frequently run out of breath. Take your time, enunciate carefully and fully, and finish phrases on a level note. Your audiences are 10–15 words behind you as they assimilate your message; therefore, inserting pauses helps you to be more convincing and powerful, and boosts comprehension. And don't forget to smile when you speak, as it resonates in your voice. It conveys warmth and confidence.

When you deliver a boardroom or a podium speech, know what you are going to say, and begin with the end in mind. When you get to the point, everyone gets your point. When a message wanders, so do minds, and you want to keep your audiences firmly focused on you.

Listen carefully to the voices of successful women in your circle. Are they mellifluous, moderated, and mellow? Do you gain confidence by listening to them? If so, draw inspiration from them and then work on your own voice (don't copy, be your authentic self).

Women are using their voices to speak out and speak up for justice all around the globe. We hear from environmental activists, women in political office, and women who are fighting for the rights of their fellow citizens.

Women are increasingly taking leadership roles; thus, their voices are vital tools. Women are standing up, speaking up, and demanding to be heard. Of course, there is no "right way" to speak, but our messages should be amplified by our voices, not weakened.

Remember: your voice is your logo, your product, and your brand. It is unique, just as the message you deliver has never been heard before with your words and tone. Your voice can make a positive change in our world!

Made in the USA
Las Vegas, NV
10 December 2021